Interpreting Basic Theology

Addison H. Leitch

INTERPRETING

BASIC

THEOLOGY

CHANNEL PRESS, INC. · GREAT NECK · NEW YORK

INTERPRETING BASIC THEOLOGY

Copyright © 1961 by Channel Press

PREFACE

THIS BOOK ORIGINATED IN A SERIES OF STUDIES FOR a Teachers' Quarterly called "The Earnest Worker," one chapter appearing each month during the year 1955. Later, the substance of several of the chapters was used in a series of studies given as a part of a program of the United Presbyterian Men's meeting at Green Lake, Wisconsin, in April of 1956. Dr. Lee Edwin Walker's suggestion at the meeting that the studies be printed in book form led to the preparation and publication of *Beginnings in Theology,* now out of print.

The present volume is an expansion and reworking of the twelve chapters of the original book, with three new chapters added. The new title, INTERPRETING BASIC THEOLOGY, is designed both to encourage the out-and-out newcomer to the field of theology and to reflect the dynamic nature of the learning process.

Perhaps the purpose of this book is described best

by some words of W. J. B. Martin, that delightful columnist of "The Presbyterian Outlook," who on one occasion wrote: "I can't help thinking that we have too many theological books written by scholars for scholars, and I wish more scholars could be persuaded to write for the church instead of for their fellow professors." I am making no claims to scholarship, but my purpose in publishing this book is to address myself to those who have not pursued theology in any formal or scholarly fashion. These are "first steps" in theology. We all have to start somewhere, and since I believe theology is the most interesting (as it is the most valuable) study available to any of us, I am hopeful that this simple treatment of a series of doctrines will help many to get started in theological reading and study.

The book is so designed that it need not be read from cover to cover—indeed, I think the opening chapters are the most difficult ones—for each chapter is treated as a study in itself. Some will find the book valuable for reading and study, but for most it ought to be valuable for study groups. The chapters of chief interest to the group can be studied in any order at all.

TABLE OF CONTENTS

[7]

Chapter One

BELIEVING IN GOD

IN EVERY DISCUSSION OF GOD AND IN EVERY ATTEMPT AT definition, it is assumed that God is at least "the source, the support, and the end" of all things. He is at least that. But He is infinitely more, beyond discussion and certainly beyond exact definition. To talk about Him at all, therefore, takes us into infinity and eternity. There is thus laid on us at the outset the necessity of limiting our approach and restricting ourselves to certain directions in our thinking. In the light of such limitations we shall set ourselves to answer briefly just two questions: First, Why do men believe in God? Second, What do they believe?

Why, then, do men believe in God? They believe in God, quite simply, because they have to. The belief in some kind of a god is found everywhere and always, limited by neither time nor place. Wherever you find men you find men believing in a god. This kind of belief is so universal that most scholars have concluded that such belief must be a part of man's very nature, an inescapable part of his being. This is not to say that men are able to analyze their beliefs or that they are able to state their beliefs clearly in order to share them with someone else, or that all men everywhere believe the same things about God. This belief in God, furthermore, is not always the result of thinking about Him, but is usually a starting place from which men think about all other things.

Belief in God is clear to men, as is their belief in their own existence; a man can be self-conscious, or better, conscious of himself, without ever having subjected that consciousness to analysis. But it is just because man rests in a belief in his own existence that he is prepared to understand the existence of anything else. Likewise it is just because he really believes in some kind of a god, or in the fact of a god, that he is prepared to think about things like existence, or purpose, or meaning, or value. Believing in God, therefore, is not so much the result of thinking as the starting place of thinking. Later in personal intellectual maturity, or perhaps in the maturity of the race, man gets around to analyzing the nature of his starting place. For example, a person can be seeing light through his eyes long before he understands the anatomy of the eye, and quite commonly a person can live his whole life through without ever having analyzed either his eyes or the physics of light. Nevertheless he continues to see. Even an atheist has a hard time here. Unless he is carrying on his fight against absolute nothingness, and this makes us wonder about his zeal, then he must be marshalling his arguments against something he finds ingrained in himself and in others, namely, a deep belief that needs to be shaken loose. Even his insistence that his negative arguments "make sense" is a positive appeal to some underlying sense to which all sense is somehow necessarily related.

We are living in a day when for multitudes of people the only acceptable knowledge is scientific knowledge. There are scientific men who have facts, and naïve and gullible people who have only beliefs. Scientific knowledge is true because it can be checked out in sense-experiences and in the controls of laboratory experiments. Things are true if they can be weighed, counted, and measured in three dimensions. One would hesitate to tilt with the scientific method or with those wonderful and enriching gifts of our scientists that have released us from many superstitions and given us great controls over the planet which we inhabit. What is difficult in the climate and atmosphere of our day is to point out that many things which will not subject themselves to the methods of the scientists may be true and real. What shall we say of the reality of loyalty and courage, especially the loyalty and courage of men who have been martyred as they have stood for truth? Scientists themselves have shown such heroism. We could turn aside also to discuss whether the method known as the scientific method is really, as method, the object of scientific proof or actually a belief in the value of one method and one source of data as against another. Indeed, if there be a God at all, could such a Being possibly be subjected to laboratory controls, and how, just for the sake of argument, does one measure salvation by grace alone?

For the sake of our discussion here, however, I should like to take our scientist himself, as scientist, and see whether his so-called objectivity does not really rest on belief, and on belief rooted and grounded in something or someone who can be described as God. What has already happened to the scientist before he even takes up his experiments? Does he not already carry in him a great body of belief? For one thing he has to *believe* that he is awake; and he also has to *believe* that he is alive, and even sane. These are not childish suggestions if we are going to insist on scientific proof instead of belief. As you read this page there is no way scientifically for you to prove that you are awake. This could all be last night's dream. You cannot prove that you are alive; this may well be the way the first days of your death are actually lived. You cannot prove you are sane; the people who surround you may be hired to give you the impression that what you are doing is sane, whereas you may be suffering from complete although somewhat harmless illusion. Mind you, I believe that you are alive and awake and sane, and you believe it too, and unless we both believe it, there is no reason for us to continue this discussion, or any other for that matter. But notice the word which has forced its way into our discussion—the word "believe." You see, unless you "believe" these things about yourself and others there is no use moving on to reasons, or proofs, however objective they may appear. We have to "believe" first. Then we can get on with our business, even the business of scientific research.

The scientist, therefore, goes into his laboratory believing these first truths about himself and his confreres. But he has more serious beliefs. Not only is he alive and awake and sane, but he believes also that there is Truth (spelled with a capital T) and Reason (spelled with a capital R). What he finds in the laboratory will have to have a relatedness to everything else; no item can stand by itself. He believes in a *Uni*verse of Truth. What he finds will have to "make sense," or "stand to reason," and he will be holding to his belief in Reason undergirding necessarily all our reasonings. Moreover his search will be worth while (which is a value judgment, not a scientific datum) and if he is to be a "good" scientist he will have to be an "honest" scientist (and these are moral judgments). Just for the sake of pondering the nature of things, why does science have to be "honest"; why does morality lie beneath good science?

Truth, Reason, Morality—these undergird scientific method. These are beliefs *from* which we move, not the objects of research *to* which we move. They are what thinkers have come to define as "first truths." Already we can see them as descriptive of God. Belief in *something* like God, belief in *someone* like God, begins to sound like a necessity.

Take the subject of Truth. The scientists in research laboratories today, and there are thousands of them, hold one belief in common; that there is Truth to be found. All truth has to have some relationship to every other truth, and all truths must be grounded finally in Truth. Einstein's greatest discovery, greater even than relativity, lay in the statement in an equation of the relationship between matter and energy. Matter and energy *must* be related in some way, you see, so he had to search out the secret. But why *must* they? This pressure of the *must* is what drives men in their research. The movements of the electrons around their protons and the movements of the stars in their courses—is there some common law for the microcosm and for the macrocosm? Why must there be one common law for little things as for big things?

What is a man saying when he exclaims, "Why, it stands to reason!" or "Why, that doesn't make sense!" He is insisting that there is a Reason underlying all reasons to which his reasons and my reasons must be in some way related. An idea doesn't just float around; it needs grounding. Grounding in what? Are we not insisting on a ground-work of Reason, something that makes sense, some point of reference that will give meaning and cohesion to all our thinking, so that what we think can be shared with what other people think? The mathematicians see this plainly, for they insist on total systems of mathematics—and nothing, not one thing, can get out of line. It is worth considering how the correct mathematics in your mind demands correct mathematics in my mind, and both of us find the very same scheme of things when we search the heavens with a telescope. There is a kind of restlessness in our minds until any bit of information finds its resting place in the total Sense of things.

But what message would aliens send that could be understood by earthlings? Dr. Drake suggests a familiar series of numbers, such as 1, 2, 3, 4. Professor Purcell believes that a simple on-off signal would be more logical as a starter. After that the messages could progress to *mathematical relationships, which are surely the same in all planetary systems. . . .*[1]

Shift this kind of thinking over to the realm of values. One thing, we insist, is better than another. Even if you criticize my statements at this point it is because you believe that what a man says *ought* to be true! And how can we know that one thing is better than another thing unless we have some conception of the idea of Best? Good, better, best—but we can know *better* over *good* only in terms of *best*. We admit, of course, that there are many relative values and endless personal and racial

---

[1] "Science—Project OZMA," *Time,* April 18, 1960, p. 53. (Italics added for emphasis.)

customs, but the idea of the best constantly haunts us, and it is very foolish to pretend it isn't there. It is a nice question, therefore: whence comes this idea of the best? Also a sense of "oughtness" forces its way in here, a moral demand which is also inescapable. If we know the better we ought to choose the better. Why? There is deep necessity here. Just as surely as we cannot escape the sense of *must* in our search for Truth or for Reason, so we cannot escape that same sense of *must* in discovering what matters most in life and what we *ought* to be doing about it. Reason, Truth, Value, Morality—something like God—force themselves into our beliefs.

To the extent, therefore, that we can accept certain underlying beliefs as the starting place for all other beliefs—and in fact, all other action—to that extent we are led to a belief in God as First Truth. Many have found this approach completely satisfying to them. Others have been led to believe in God by starting the whole question at the other end of the line. They look at the world about them and find evidences for the existence of God by starting where they are. What they find in the created world is looked upon as "proof," after the manner of the scientists, for God. Such "proofs" for the existence of God are very old ones. They have been subjected to much criticism and therefore to considerable refinement in the history of thought. In spite of criticism, in one form or another, they keep cropping up in men's thinking, one argument appealing to one generation more than another, but none of the arguments ever disappearing. Such durability probably points to their strength; the arguments give external support to what we have already discovered as internal necessities in the workings of men's minds.

Arguments for God's existence, reasons from the world of external evidence for believing in God, have taken on the following descriptive titles: Cosmological, Teleological, Anthropological, and Ontological. We do not need to burden you with these names, but it is necessary to understand what the names signify, and to see how the arguments are constructed. Very simply they all follow the same scheme: any effect must have a cause capable of producing the effect.

Start with the easiest, the *Cosmological* argument. The root-word that helps us is "cosmos"—the universe; what Lewis calls "the whole show." Just look at the whole universe and ask this simple question: "How come?" Indeed yes! "How come?" Birds, bees, rocks, clouds, stars, atmosphere—here they all are. How did they get here? This argument states that this "whole show" must be accounted for by some cause equal to the task of bringing it into existence and keeping it going. That first cause, whatever it is, must be at least as big as the thing it has produced and must have the power also of its production, big enough to get the whole thing under way. What cause is big enough for this?

The *Teleological* argument looks at the universe a

little more closely and sees its intricate and amazing design. Now we look at the structure of a leaf, the growth of a seed, the power of capillary attraction, the stars in their course. Design and purpose seem interrelated in everything about us. Infinite design demands an infinite Designer. There is a mind at work here with creativity and a plan. *From* something, something *comes*. Can we possibly account for design in the universe without a controlling designing mind? Does a watch "just happen" without a watchmaker? Do things just happen? *Can* they just happen? As has been asked many times: How long would it take ten thousand monkeys hammering on ten thousand typewriters (and monkeys and typewriters would have to be accounted for first) to "just happen" to write the plays of Shakespeare?

One of the most amazing designs in the universe is man himself. How can we account for him? The question sets in motion the *Anthropological* argument. What cause is equal to the fact of man? Man is a person and has what we call personality; are we going to insist that he has come from an impersonal source? Man is creative in so many ways; was the source of his existence uncreative? Are Bach and Beethoven, DaVinci and Michelangelo the accidental by-products of an accidental process that began when the primordial slime (wherever that came from) accidentally gathered together to produce the first living cell? Did accidental impersonal process produce persons, persons like Bach?

The *Ontological* argument points to perfection. Several forms of the argument have appeared in the history of thought, but that of Descartes is perhaps the clearest. Starting with the idea of perfection, an idea resident in a man's mind, Descartes raises the question as to where this idea of perfection has its source. It cannot be produced from the universe that has in it many imperfections. It cannot come from man for he makes no claims for perfection in himself; the idea of perfection is actually his ideal for himself. Whence this idea if not from man or from the external world? There must be another source; the idea has been implanted by some perfect one. This could only be God.

When we take the first reasons for believing in God, the arguments from first truths, we have an answer for our first question: "Why do men believe in God?" This is answering our question with what are called *a priori* arguments. Men believe something about God as ultimate Truth and Reason and Goodness. On the other hand, when we examine the evidence around us we are reasoning *a posteriori,* and we reason from an examination of the universe to God's might, from the design and purpose of the universe to God's intelligence, from the nature of man in person and personality to the personality and creativity of God; and in searching for our ideas of perfection we are led to seek the source and ground of perfection in a perfect God. We have, therefore, rational, although not final, reasons for believing in God, and we have rational, although not final, reasons for knowing something about the God in whom we believe. We know from all our discussion that there must be a God of Truth, Reason, and Goodness who is mighty, intelligent, personal, creative and perfect. How much more do we need? But, praise God, there is even more!

One of the wonders of life is how our searchings find answers moving out to meet us. Thirst finds water, and water would not be nearly so delightful did we not thirst first. The need and the answer fit in ways we might not have invented ourselves. Hunger is answered with food and with true hunger the food has zest and interest. Our loves find fulfillment in the beloved. "Can a man by searching find out God?" Only finally and completely when God comes out to meet him and to answer his questions; only when God wills to reveal Himself. Revealed religion means this at least: man's search for God is God already coming and seeking him. And the proof for a revealed religion is finally this: does it in the last analysis answer man's deepest questions? And beyond this even, sometimes revealed religion can lead men beyond their own deepest questions to create in their hearts new and more profound questions of the spirit.

What then can men believe about God? Only what he is pleased to reveal. The heavens declare his glory;

there are things which all can know from his creation of his "power and divinity"; there is a light "which lighteth every man coming into the world." But more than this, God has been pleased to give a revelation of Himself in his Word and we can believe in the living Word who is there set forth. Just as we come to know our friends by their clothes, by their walk, their appearance, the sound of their voices, and yet never really know them beyond their willingness to reveal to us their true natures, so with God. All our reasoning about Him gives us only broken lights of Him until He gives us his light; we are, as Calvin suggests, like men who see but who need the "divine spectacles" of God's Word before all things are brought into focus.

In the Scriptures we find what God has told us of Himself through the revelation of His acts and the revelation of His will and the revelation of His truth —by spoken words, by holy history, by mighty acts— and in these last days "he has spoken to us in his Son." When we see Jesus we see the Father, and the Holy Spirit "takes of the things of Christ and shows them unto us" and the promise goes beyond all our imaginings about knowledge, the knowledge of God, for in the last days "we shall even be like him, for we shall see him as he is." In Christ Jesus we see and handle the Word of Life.

Chapter Two

THE TRINITY

IN HIS REVELATION OF HIMSELF GOD HAS TAUGHT US two things about Himself: there is just one God, and there are three persons in the Godhead. This is easy to say but very difficult to understand. In our brief statement of faith, called the Apostles' Creed, we have repeated over and over again that we believe in God "the Father . . . and in Jesus Christ his only Son our Lord . . . the Holy Ghost." Other ancient and more extensive statements of the church are more detailed and explicit in affirming that there is this one God who is three persons. We are familiar with other formularies as when, for example, we hear the words of a benediction: "Grace, mercy and peace, from God the Father, the Son, and the Holy Spirit . . ." The great commission in the Gospel according to Matthew directs us to baptize "in the name of the Father, the Son, and the Holy Spirit." We therefore have universal agreement in Christendom that we have one God

—we are monotheists—but that we know God as three persons, Father, Son, and Holy Spirit. Repeating these creeds and accepting these words make the ideas clear enough; the trouble is that we have before us what looks like a logical impasse. A man can say these things, but how can a man really believe that it is even possible to talk about one and more than one as the same thing at the same time?

It will help if we understand three things at the outset. First, this whole idea of the Trinity is not something the church thought up just to make things difficult. We are tempted to believe that something can be more "religious" if it is more mysterious. The English schoolboy is quoted as saying, "Faith is believing something when you know it isn't so," and many people exercise their faith in this fashion. "Say whatever has to be said in church," they seem to say. "It is in a different compartment of life from ordinary living, so one believes it in a different sort of way. It isn't the kind of thing that has to stand up, so to speak, in a barbershop conversation or in street-corner philosophizing." Such an attitude about our beliefs is deadly, and especially so in Protestantism. We are to walk by faith; we are to live out what we really believe; therefore, in some measure, we must understand our beliefs as sensible and rational, and in some way applicable to life as we live it or life as we ought to live it. The problem of the Trinity is forced on us by the Bible record, and the Bible declares in the most forceful fashion (without putting the ideas together) that there is one God and only one God. Then the Bible proceeds to speak of the Father as God, the Son as God, the Holy Spirit as God. The creeds of the church have been true to these great affirmations, not in creating the intellectual puzzle but in making certain that what the Bible says about God, we too must say about God. When the basic statements are before us, clearly and cleanly, then we can puzzle out how such things can be possible and believable. The church has not invented this structure of belief; it has only been trying to make statements that are true to the record.

In the second place, once the idea of the Trinity is grasped we are able to sense that in some measure this is the way God would have to be, because, in fact, this is the way He seems to reveal Himself. In the most natural way we recognize that there must be a creator of all things; then this creative life shows itself physically in the world around us; then there seems to be an empowering of the Spirit in the spirit of man. Such things about God can be sensed in just the general observation of the world around us and in contemplating God's ways with men. This is only a kind of general revelation; the written revelation of Scripture gives us our clue by saying that there is a Creator, the Father; that there is a physical revealing, the Son; that there is a Spirit who touches our spirits. I have no desire to press this point at this stage in our discussion except to say in the most general way that if the structure of the Trinity is rightly sensed by us it ought to give us some clue to reality, because, after all, the ultimate and final reality on which all things are based is God, and what He really is ought to show in His created world and in His relationship to it.

In the third place—and we have been edging in this direction all the time—whatever God reveals of Himself is after all, a revelation. It would seem, therefore, would it not, that if the Scripture record concerning God is correct, if God is as God is there described—one God in three persons—then this revelation, mysterious as it may appear, is actually given to us not as a puzzle but as a guide. The Trinity therefore is not so much an object of our study and search for understanding in itself as it is a revelation of truth about all other things. In other words we should make an about-face; instead of taking this world about us as a thing completely understood and in the light of such simplicities forcing God into our ordinary logic, we should rather take God as the source and ground of all existence and come to an understanding of the mysteries of this universe from the truth in Him. Put it this way: if the triune God is final Truth, then all truths must finally rest in Him; conversely, God, the Truth, cannot be subjected to the truths which we have thus far mastered. We shall understand the truth about our world from God's nature; we shall not understand God from our limited understanding of the apparent nature of this world.

Our next step now is to hold fast to this last idea: the triune God, as revealed, is a revelation of the true nature of all things. He is not the puzzle but the clue.

One of the oldest problems in human thought has been this very problem, the relation of the one to the many, the one to the more-than-one. About six hundred years before Christ, what we know as Western thought had its beginnings. Men posed for themselves a gigantic question: what is the nature of the Real? Or again, What is the nature of ultimate reality? In a sense they were asking, from the standpoint of philosophy, What is the nature of God? All kinds of theories were brought forward. Thales had the thoughtful suggestion that Reality is water. Why? Well, water has the three forms of solid, liquid and gas; all living things have water; there is more water in the world than anything else. Reality must be water. Another thinker suggested fire because it is both dynamic and static, because it seems to be both Being and Becoming, two basic characteristics of all reality. Another thinker suggested a kind of atomic structure of reality, with atoms falling through space and joining together or falling apart, thus producing things as they are for a few aeons of time and then disintegrating and joining together in other structures as time passed on. Thus the theories; and they all had some merit.

In the search for Reality, however, another question kept pressing for an answer. Whenever the theorists thought of the last and final thing, whether water or fire or falling atoms, they discovered that the thing itself was always more than itself. In other words, water not only had to be water but it had to be a power which was not water in order that there could be the power for water to turn into something else. It is all well and good to say that water or fire or anything else is the ultimate and final reality, but what about the power? Power and water are not the same thing; nevertheless, if a thing like water is the ground and source of all things, a thing like water (a single substance) must be more than just water; it must be water plus the power to turn itself into something else. From the standpoint of philosophy, at least, the one always seemed in its oneness to be necessarily more than one. Singleness appeared to be necessarily complex.

Lest you think this is the kind of dreamy thing only philosophers in ancient Miletus would worry about on a lazy summer day, take a fresh look at what the physicists are telling us today about the structure of reality as they examine the physical world which they see. The idea of a material world made of little blocks of matter has long since disappeared. Molecules have been discovered to be dynamic complexes of other bits of matter which in turn are characterized by relationships more than by singleness. In any case, once you get to talking about protons and electrons you have to take your probe deeper into mesons, and the end is not yet. One thing in our observations is perfectly clear, however; whatever the size of this last bit of matter, this last bit of matter is always matter which is energized. The thing in itself is always more than itself. Singleness has complexity and is even more complex because it is always in relationship to something else. In this mysterious universe of the physicist we find what the revelation of God has already told us: wherever you find oneness you will always find more than one, and you will find dynamic relationship. The Trinity was already a description of this before the physicists discovered it.

Or try the psychologists. The Gestalt approach, recognition of the total person (and it was first the Old Testament approach), is a clue to the understanding of man to which we have come in this day. There is no use making a man all body, as the behaviorists tried. Or all spirit, as a Hindu might argue. Or to break a man up into certain faculties like cognition, affection and volition. Man has faculties, sure enough; there is no question that the body is as real as real can be; but we have to accept the fact also that there is a whole not-body reality in man; we do not confuse his brain with his thought. But for all that, he is a man, a total structure, and whereas we may study him from this angle or from that angle, take him apart for the sake of anaylsis, we come to understand him and deal with him correctly only when we deal with the total man—Body-Mind, or if you will, Body-Mind-

Spirit. The body is not the Mind and the Mind is not the Body. No one maintains that anymore.

But how the two get together in one person—there's the rub. Yet they *are* together. As long ago as Descartes, there was serious speculation about the switching point between body and mind. How does thought become physical action? How do physical experiences become thought? How is food digested in such a way as to feed muscles and energize spirit? How does one thing that is the opposite of another thing nevertheless weld together with that other thing in such completion that we have a new totality, a single being? One thing is once again more than one.

While we are thus engaged in a little amateur psychologizing, another observation may prove interesting: the structure of the mind itself, especially in what we call self-consciousness. I know myself to be one person and I have an awareness of self as over against all other selves and all other things. I am not split, I am not a schizoid; I am one single person. Nevertheless I have the power, in so far as I understand myself, to "take myself in hand." I subject myself to self-praise or self-criticism. But who, I ask, in an experience like that, is talking to whom? Self-examination is an amazing faculty of the mind, especially the mind of a person who is just one single person! The so-called single items in life are much more complex than we thought. But then the revelation of the nature of Reality in the nature of God has already told us that.

The problem of the One and the Many in philosophy, the mystery of matter and energy in physics, the body-mind structure in persons, the powers of the mind in self-examination, these all point up the deeper mysteries of existence and in their apparent paradox are akin to the problem we have been facing in the Trinity. We become increasingly aware that the deeps of life are illustrating the deeps of God. That the Trinity —one God, three persons—appears paradoxical, therefore, becomes no argument against it whatsoever. It is the sort of thing we should expect if we look upward toward the reality of God or downward toward the realities of this planet.

Once we accept the structure of the Trinity and understand how instructive this can be in other areas of thought, we go on to discover what the Trinity has to say about relationships. This has already been hinted at in the dynamics of atom structure; however, we want to think about it here more in the area of human relationships. The church fathers refined their definition to the point where they could warn us against two things in our understanding of the Trinity: we must not divide the essence (we have only one God) and we must not confuse the persons (our one God is triune). Whatever this oneness is—and the essence must not be divided—it is never oneness in the sense that the persons are lost. Life and relationship characterize the inner existence of God. As has been suggested many times: God is love; love needs an object. God's love is complete somehow within the life of the Godhead itself. There are persons, and there are therefore relationships.

Some of the grand unities of our faith depend on the possibility of such relationships of many individuals in oneness. The unity is complete, nevertheless the relationship is never such that the persons are lost. "I and the Father are One," says Christ; or again, "He that hath seen me hath seen the Father." We are accepting this kind of truth in our acceptance of the Trinity. But what shall we say of something like this: "It is no longer I that live but Christ liveth in me," or "For me to live is Christ." Union with Christ is one of the grand themes of the New Testament. Whatever Paul means by this union, however, he does not mean that he, Paul, is lost. No, he is enhanced! The union is complete, yet in such wonderful fashion that Paul is more than Paul could possibly have been without that union.

Take this on another step. In the Intercessory Prayer of John 17 we are looking in on some of the unities of the Godhead. What can we possibly say of the intercession of the twenty-first verse: ". . . as thou Father art in me, and I in thee, that they also may be one in us." We are to be caught up somehow into the very person of God! But this is no Hindu concept of being lost in the All. The grand truth about the grand unities of our faith is this: there is true oneness, and yet we never confuse the persons. Our fulfillment is to be in God, but it is still *our* fulfillment that we shall experience.

One of Paul's favorite illustrations is that of the human body, where he delights in the unity in diversity, the diversity in unity. We are instructed by Jesus in his picture of the vine and branches. Husband and wife, we are told, become one, but never a oneness in the sense that he becomes less man and she less woman. On the contrary, their characteristics are enhanced and fulfilled. There are unities of lovers, of friends, of families, of churches, of believers with their Lord, and so with one another. The unities can be real and complete, and the persons are not lost. We shall never divide the essence, and we must never confuse the persons. All this has already been revealed to us in the Trinity. The Trinity is the ultimate clue, not the ultimate puzzle. He shall yet teach us the grand unities of races and of nations.

Some people are further helped in their understanding of the Trinity by the use of comparisons and analogies. This is good practice so long as we also understand that no analogy can be a complete description or definition. One analogy frequently used is the three-leafed clover—one plant with three parts. But we see immediately what the trouble is here. The clover has three parts but the three parts are not one, so our analogy falls to the ground. A helpful analogy is that of the sun in the sky. The sun has its lodgement in the heavens; it reveals itself in the light on earth; it works in the energies of the heat which we cannot see. Thus we have only one thing, located in a given place, made known to us visibly (this would be the Word made flesh) and energizing us with unseen power (this would be the Spirit). The illustration serves us in making clear how one thing is known through another, but it would be hard to say that the heat of the sun is fully sun, as we say that the Spirit of God is fully God.

Another helpful analogy describes a woman in her three functions as daughter, wife and mother. She is only one person but exhibits her self in three different ways or "modes" (some would call this modalism). Her father knows her as daughter, her husband as his wife, her son as his mother. It is not that she "turns on," so to speak, one aspect or another of her being. She remains just "herself," but in her variety of relationships she is known in three different ways. If you can picture her sitting at table at the evening meal, perhaps her thoughts turned inward on private contemplation, you will recognize that her father, husband and son are reacting to her in three different ways, "knowing" her in a particular "office."

Dorothy Sayers in her *Mind of the Maker* uses the analogy of the creative artist as he "makes" something, illustrating for us how God the Maker does His creative work. If the artist is a painter then what he has to say becomes "flesh," and dwells among us on his canvas; that is, the thought that is within him is made known in the painting. Then people observe the work of art. Finally one observer really "sees" the picture, for he is caught up in a singleness of spirit with the creative artist. The parallel is very interesting when worded this way, having as it does some echoes of Biblical language—for the onlooker, being touched by the spirit of the artist, has the things of the artist shown to him, and when he sees the picture he finally sees through the picture to the creative idea itself. The Spirit takes of the things of Christ and shows them unto us and when we have seen Christ we have seen the Father, and through the Word made flesh we do not so much know the Word as we come to know God himself.

So much for analogies. It is not likely that any human analogy will do more than help us along the way, show us how the Trinity is possible and rational and believable. Many years ago in his discussion of what he called antinomies, Immanuel Kant made perfectly clear to us that there are limitations to our finite minds and that with these limitations we can contemplate but not engulf things which are infinite. This is not to say that what we know is not true; it is to say that what we know is not complete. Arithmetic is true as far as it goes but it does not go all the way to calculus; at the same time it is a true step in the right direction.

As the writer of Ecclesiastes has said, "He has written eternity in our hearts." Man at creation was "inbreathed" with the breath of God. Thus the yearning after infinity is always in us. We cannot master the infinities and by the same token we cannot leave them alone. They are beyond us, but in some way they are akin to us. We shall indeed some day come face to face. Our great God draws us on to know, and someday "we shall know even as we are fully known."

Chapter Three

THE BIBLE: THE WORD OF GOD

THE BIBLE IS THE WORD OF GOD. IN SOME WAY THAT statement is believed and maintained by Christians everywhere. Some hold that the very words of the Bible are the very words of God. By this they mean that in the originals we have in some sense "divine originals," actual words spoken by God through his servants, the prophets. Others hold that the actual words of Scripture, either in the originals or in the translations, are of secondary importance; what is really important is the thought the words convey, i.e., the "sense" of Scripture. These would hold that what we want is not the *words* of God but the *Word* of God which comes through the medium of the words. Others tell us that the Bible is a means of conveying to men the *Living Word,* even Jesus Christ, and that we understand the *words* of the Bible and the *Word* of the Bible only insofar as the *Living Word* is sealed in our hearts. Others go so far as to say that there is no word of God until out of the words of the Bible the Living Word becomes alive in us; *the total process* of words to life makes of the Bible the Word of God. There is truth in every one of these positions and we need to understand how this is so.

Let me use a simple illustration. Let us suppose that a man wants to say "I love you" (and this is clearly one of the things God is saying to us in Scripture). In how many ways can this be said? In the seventeenth century, Shah Jahan wanted to tell the world of his love for his wife, so he had built the Taj Mahal. In a beautiful building he told the world and all succeeding generations of the profundity and purity of his love. Another kind of artist, Franz Liszt, wrote a love song called *Liebestraum;* he gave his message of love through music. When Elizabeth Browning wrote her *Sonnets from the Portuguese* she was telling Robert Browning of her love, especially in that matchless sonnet which begins, "How do I love thee, let me count the ways . . ." She was saying "I love you" in poetry. Shah Jahan spoke in stone; Liszt spoke in music; Elizabeth Browning spoke in poetry.

There are so many ways of speaking. Multitudes of people incapable of any arts are nevertheless able to find ways of telling others that they love them in countless deeds of thoughtfulness. A man delights to tell a woman that he loves her; he delights even more when he discovers that he can show her in loving acts, in the living word, so to speak, that he truly does love her. A love relationship is sustained by words and living words, and there are endless and delightful ways of saying this one simple message.

What we have said thus far then is that there are many ways of saying "I love you." However, once an artist has chosen his medium for the communication of his message, he is forced into the disciplines of the particular art of his choice. If an artist has chosen to speak through music, then he must not only master music as his means of expression, but he must also accept the fact that he is limited by the nature of the medium he has chosen. To put it another way, he will find it impossible to convey his message through music according to the laws of architecture; he cannot speak in architecture according to the laws of poetry. There are, of course, great riches in the medium of his choice; there are also disciplines and laws and limitations. There are things he can do and there are things he cannot do. If we can suppose him to be a perfect artist we can then suppose that he will know exactly *how* to say exactly *what* he wants to say in obedience to his chosen art and its possibilities. His exactitude here, in small things as in great, will be a measure of his mastery; he will never be careless about the disciplines of his art. Bach is most nearly perfect in music because he is most nearly law-abiding within the disciplines of his art.

Now let us turn to another illustration before we

turn back to the Bible. Wagner was a great contemporary of Liszt. It was said of him, and I think he said it of himself, that he could appreciate a piece of music best by simply reading the score. He claimed that having the instruments of the orchestra between him and the music was an extra interference between him and the full understanding and enjoyment of the composer. Beethoven, literally unable to hear, also nevertheless "heard" every note he saw on a score. Toscanini had this ability. I can believe that this was possible for Beethoven and Toscanini and Wagner, although it is quite impossible for me.

At any rate, let us suppose that Wagner is reading the score of *Liebestraum* by Liszt. Liszt has written the score; he has written such and such notes, and not other notes; he has written music and not poetry; he has wanted to say something definite about love, and this is the way he has said it, this is the means of his message. We can argue that it could have been said differently or might even have been said better, either by some other artist or perhaps even by Liszt himself. But we are limited entirely by what Liszt did say; these are his notes. If Wagner wants to know what Liszt has to say, he had better give attention to Liszt's notes, to all of them; the accidentals in this case are not accidental! And Wagner will not fill in, nor correct, nor expunge. More than that Wagner will want to look at Liszt's own score if at all possible; he prefers the original. To be true to the Word that Liszt

[39]

wants to convey he will have to find the exact notes in which Liszt conveyed that Word.

Now we can build the illustration a little. Suppose Wagner wants to perform Liszt's *Liebestraum* before an audience in order that others may receive what it is that Liszt is saying. He may choose a string quartet, or he will rewrite the original for a symphony orchestra (and he must decide what constitutes a full symphony orchestra, and where all the players shall sit), or he may write variations for the piano. Somehow, and this is the test of his own artistry, he must interpret to his audience what Liszt has to say and, insofar as he is able, he must be absolutely true to what Liszt has himself said; the original by Liszt will be his constant point of reference, his control. And what will be the result? The people in the audience will know what Liszt has said; they may be led to go back and examine the way in which he said it in his original score and thus be further enriched; but most of all the word of Liszt will be in their hearts, a new song in their hearts, perhaps. This whole process may be repeated again and again, and succeeding generations may have similar experiences as this Word of Liszt is conveyed to them in their day, and men may well tell others of what Liszt has said to them. But whenever it is said, and however it is said, some men will always have a first concern with *how* Liszt said it in the first place. They will eventually miss his message if they become careless about his original score. And if the original is ever lost, then men will be concerned to reproduce that original as faithfully as possible from all the available copies at hand.

The parallel is clear enough; we are ready now to say some things about the Bible, and we shall try to say some things which are even beyond the limitations of our illustration.

God *so* loved the world, and He has said so. How has He said so? We can read the Prot-Evangel in the third chapter of Genesis, the fifty-third chapter of Isaiah, or the twenty-third Psalm. Or listen to such words as these: "Let not your heart be troubled," or again, "Come unto me all ye that labor and are heavy laden," or these wondrous words: "My grace is sufficient," and that final word, "And God shall wipe away all tears from their eyes; and there shall be no more death, neither sorrow, nor crying, neither shall there be any more pain. . . ." The Bible says many things about many subjects, but let us concentrate on just this one message: God is love. Let us suppose that this is the only message. In how many ways, then, can God say this? The possibilities are endless. But the Bible binds us up to this: God has said it, and He has chosen to say it in certain ways. If we want to know truly what it is that God has said, then we must examine the ways in which He has chosen to say it. As we cannot be true to a composer's music without being faithful to his notes, so we cannot know what it is that God is saying or has said unless we submit ourselves to the way in which He Himself has chosen to say it.

Now we are back to our starting place—words, Word, Living Word, Life. How is God's word communicated? Like this. God has spoken in times past "by divers portions and in divers manner," and in these last days "he hath spoken to us in his Son." Such ways God has chosen. We want to know then, first of all, what he actually said and how He said it. We are forced, therefore, to being concerned about the originals. We know, of course, that He spoke "in the prophets." This was a medium chosen by Him thus giving Him possibilities and limitations. We may be sure that He was master of His medium (He created the prophets whom He used) so that the prophets, even in their own peculiarities of thought and speech, could be used by Him to communicate his message. We seek out the originals, therefore, because however differently He may have said things through His chosen prophets as against how *we* might have said things through prophets of our choice. Once the message was spoken His way, *that's the way it was said*. The thing stands written. We cannot tamper with that original and be true to the message; we must find it, or recreate it as perfectly as possible from all the translations and versions that lie at hand. Such research goes on endlessly because men believe that it matters what was said in the "originals."

This is probably a good place to refer back to some of the "accidentals" in the music of Liszt. Liszt's music is too flamboyant for some, full of graces and extras which make some people think him to have been a show-off. He was, of course, an amazing virtuoso himself, and probably wrote more notes in some of his compositions than most performers could use. But, you see, this *characterizes* his music; this conveys his kind of message over the quiet control, say, of Brahms. The so-called "extras" in his music are what make his music. We knew a painter in our family who attained some stature in the world of art. He criticized himself by saying that he never attained the greatness he should have liked because he could never quit painting a picture; he was always adding a touch here and another touch there. But in spite of his own self-criticism, these extra touches were his art, his way of doing things, his way of saying things. You knew the man and his message by these little, but not necessarily insignificant, details.

What shall we say then of how God reveals Himself? We know that "the heavens declare the glory of God." How do the heavens declare that glory? Well, sunsets are beautiful, I am told, because of dust in the air; the beauty of the moon is not really marred by markings on the face that might look ghastly if we examined them too closely; "one star differs from another star in glory"; the majestic message of a mountain range is not destroyed because the face of the mountain is covered with bits and pieces of broken shale and twisted trees. What may look like an extra, or an error, or a smudge, or a fault on close examination, may from another viewpoint

[43]

be seen as necessary to the whole picture. An artist uses these touches to get his complete effects.

And in our examination of the Scriptures, our close-up view may well reveal what looks to us like discrepancy, or an item of indifference, or even utter foolishness. But maybe we need another look. It was the broken, bloody, beaten, fly-covered, crucified Nazarene who was revealing the love of God, and that to the uttermost. Our dainty pedantic exactitudes are not always the tools for an artist. God can say exactly what He wants to say in unexpected ways. The great B. B. Warfield described how God uses His prophets as an architect uses stained glass in a cathedral. There is light to be communicated through glass; the architect's artistry is in his mastery of the glass to communicate exactly the kind of light he wants. But the glass he chooses may well be bent, uneven, and certainly opaque.

We give attention then to exactly what was said, resisting the temptation to discard what doesn't suit us, *because we respect the artist*. But when we know what has been said, and when we have approached as closely as possible what has been said, this must then be put over into a language which can be used. The Aramaic and Hebrew and Greek must be made available in English and French and Japanese and Russian.

Our original score is ready now for a string quartet or a pipe organ. Then most of us need interpretation. This is where the preacher comes in. To get God's message, he must examine the original languages as far back as he can get toward those originals. Then he must interpret what has been said, just as the conductor of an orchestra interprets his score, and one preacher is better than another preacher only as he rightly interprets in relevancy and in power what was once-and-for-all given.

Now we have the listener. The Word of God was spoken and it now stands written; and now the preacher has spoken; and the word is finally speaking to the listener's condition. What does it speak? It speaks God's Word to him and to his need; to his neighbor it will say the same thing, but will also say something different, different to suit the difference in his particular life. And if the wonderful words of life have really moved the listeners, they will receive with the Word something of strength, assurance, judgment, grace, the bread and water of life. But both preacher and listener will still be bound to the Bible for their original sources and resources; and in the last analysis the Word will come alive only as it has been true to the words.

As we come to the conclusion of this too brief treatment, we must point out that our analogies and illustrations in the arts, and especially in music, are helpful but not complete. In the message of the Bible many media are being used even in the medium of the written words. In the Bible we have not only straightforward messages but also poetry, proverb, history, biography, and finally, Jesus Christ, the Living Word, about whom other words are written in Scripture, and who himself was speaking certain words, the "words of eternal life."

[45]

One needs the Holy Spirit as interpreter, one needs teachers and preachers; one needs commentaries and helps; one needs to bring the riches of his experiences in life; one needs a hungering and thirsting for the bread and water of life. Never this side of eternity can we write finality on what God has said and is saying to us on any subject, through the Scriptures.

One other word. When we are calling the Bible "the Word of God," we are also being careful to say that it is inspired by the Spirit of God in a way that no other writing can claim, no other writing does claim. Liszt, Browning, Beethoven and Milton, and all the rest, were inspired men. But here we hold to a special inspiration. I cannot believe that Isaiah did not understand about *inspiration in general*. Most men have more or less of that, and the genius has it in abundance. Isaiah, as a man, was likely a genius in his own right. But in Scripture he is trying to make something else plain, something under the heading of "Thus saith the Lord." None of the inspired writers ever explained this phenomenon to us; but they claimed it. The Bible as a whole claims it for itself; and Jesus Christ claimed it for the Scriptures and for his own words. Perhaps it was maintained but unexplained because it cannot be explained, but they all knew the difference between what they were saying under that inspiration and what they were saying apart from it. Their claims to authority are magnificent and final; our inability to define at this point should not lead us to discard the high and unique claims.

Still, with all such inspiration, God did not over-ride the person. He was master of his medium and used his medium. He said "I love you," through the words of Hosea and through the words of John, one in Hebrew and the other in Greek or possibly at times in Aramaic; but like the master artist he did not have to destroy his medium to use it. God spoke his Word in Hosea's words and in John's words and at the same time they said exactly what he wanted to have said. We cannot therefore be careless about the words, once they have been spoken.

Now we have come to the nub of the matter. How can God speak while man speaks? Well, try these examples of the interlocking of God and man: "My Father worketh until now and I work;" or this: "Work out your own salvation with fear and trembling for it is God that worketh in you;" or this "It is no longer I that live but Christ liveth in me." Inspiration is akin to this central mystery of the Christian faith: God's sovereignty working in such a way that man's responsible action is not thereby destroyed. God acts in man's actions, God through man, and both at the same time. This is great mystery and great truth. The Bible is God's Word in man's words by God's will in man's freedom.

Chapter Four

THE STRUCTURE OF MAN

"THE PROPER STUDY OF MANKIND IS MAN." SO THE POET has assured us; but what may be fine poetry can be poor theology. Theology tells us (that is, Christian theology beginning with Genesis and finding complete interpretation in Christ), that man cannot be understood in himself alone but must always be understood in relationships: relationships with God, first, and then in relationship to his fellow men, and then in relationship to the created world. Only as we understand man in his vertical relationship, i.e., toward God, can we understand man in his horizontal relationships, i.e., toward the rest of the created universe. The attempt to level off in our study of man, the attempt to refuse the God relationship, destroys all other relationships. The same old questions with the same old answers keep repeating themselves; our deepest questions are never faced; our deepest needs are never answered. Let us see how this is so.

Start by placing man in the setting of this universe. Pascal in his *Pensées* has posed the problem vividly in a variety of ways:

> Let man then contemplate the whole of nature in her full and grand majesty, and turn his vision from the low objects which surround him . . . let man consider what he is in comparison with all existence; let him regard himself as lost in this remote corner of nature; and from the little cell in which he finds himself lodged, I mean the universe, let him estimate at their true value the earth, kingdoms, cities, and himself. What is a man in the Infinite?
>
> But to show him another prodigy equally astonishing, let him examine the most delicate things he knows. . . . Let him lose himself in wonders as amazing in their littleness as the others in their vastness.
>
> For in fact what is man in nature? A Nothing in comparison with the Infinite, an All in comparison with the Nothing, a mean between nothing and everything.
>
> Our intellect holds the same position in the world of thought as our body occupies in the expanse of nature.[2]

Perhaps you have had trouble with Bible words like meekness or humility. Whatever else they mean they certainly are not to have the overtones of Casper Milquetoast. If Jesus exemplifies the Christian virtues then he must have been a meek man and a humble man.

---

[2] Pascal, *Pensées*, pp. 16-19 *passim* Everymans '31

Moses is described as a meek man and we could all gladly imitate his powers of leadership. How can we construe such ideas properly? Use Pascal's thoughts: the recognition of ourselves in the total scheme of things; this is what gives us meekness and humility. All great men have had these virtues and they are never weak virtues.

"What is man," asks the Psalmist, "that thou art mindful of him, and the son of man that thou visitest him?" What is he indeed? In terms of the universe he is nothing. On the other hand he is created "little lower than the angels;" he is "crowned," he has been given "dominion" over the works of God's hands; "thou hast put all things under his feet." It is in the recognition of his relationship to God—he is not God but man—that he has God-given status, and powers, and responsibilities. His attainments are almost endless, but they belong to man, and man is under God, and only in the reverent acceptance of that first fact, the vertical relationship, will all other relationships harmonize. We can read in Genesis 3, where the Fall is described, what ought to be evident to us without reading it, that man's false and vaunted claims for himself as god in his own right, controlling his own destiny, becoming the judge of all the earth, that man, or nation, refusing God, cannot stand. He is contrary to the true nature of things.

There are so many little touches in the Bible description of man. He is put into the garden to "dress" the garden. Contrary to popular opinion "work" as such is not a curse, but the work of man's hands is not established unless God establishes it; apart from God all his efforts can be vanity and a striving after wind. Or we note that Adam is to name the animals. That seems a simple enough sort of thing until we read the wisdom of an Aristotle who tells us that knowledge is the ability to distinguish one thing from another, to get things "named." Much of our own science of the last century, especially in biology, was the very complex problem of naming and classifying. The process still goes on; it is basic to all other kinds of knowledge. Moreover, the ability to name anything has in it some measure of control. In a sense you have to be "on top of the situation," see the whole picture, in order to say that this is this and that is that. So man was to name the creatures—the creatures did not name man! Therein was the vast difference.

Another way of recognizing this vertical relationship is to remember that man as man is always a creature. Whether a man will or will not recognize his Creator he has to start by recognizing that he is certainly not his own creator; he in no way whatsoever brings himself into existence. Whatever the forces in nature he is willing to recognize he knows that every moment of his existence depends on forces outside his own control. If he will not submit himself to God, then to whom and to what will he submit? Destiny, it seems to me, is bound up in man's recognition of God and his trust in Him, or his recognition of the forces which surround him as forces having no God-control, and his submission to these forces in a kind of hopeless abandon.

There are reasons for believing that man is a hopeless kind of creature. On a planet largely covered with water he turns out to be a land animal, depending on precious little land, too, for there is a thin and precarious layer of topsoil on minor portions of the earth on which he has to depend for his life. His children are weak and helpless, requiring constant care for many years; man is very slow to come to maturity. He cannot stand extremes of either heat or cold, of height or depth; the globe he inhabits, on which he lives such a short and frightening existence, is as nothing in the far reaches of stellar space. Man's "inhumanity to man" has been a constant in his history and he is not far, especially in these latter days, from the possibility of wiping himself off the face of the earth. All his dreams and visions seem to have within them the seeds of their own destruction; the wisest plans, given time, seem able to pervert themselves; even good customs can corrupt his world.

If we try to look at man more optimistically I am not sure that we have a better answer. Some hopeful things are true, but are they true enough and true long enough? Man has aspirations and creativity, courage to bring him back again and again; truth crushed to earth does rise again. His own self-knowledge can be a kind of brave attainment giving him the ability frequently to laugh at others and even at himself. There seems to be endless hope in him and even endless hope for him, for there is always some vestige of good in him to which one can appeal. His ideals, however hopeless, are still ideals. Buildings have been built, societies have emerged; victories have been won; the picture is not totally black.

Shall we look upon man pessimistically or optimistically? I am rather convinced by Biblical realism as against either pessimism or optimism. Here man is recognized for what he is. He is a creature who is dependent upon outside forces for his existence, contingent on multitudes of circumstances beyond his knowledge or control, a very little fellow in the midst of a very big universe. But the forces are God's forces and this creature is God's creature, and the promises are God's promises, and in obedience, in recognition of his creaturehood, this man has destiny and sonship. He is dependent, but he is dependent on a living Creator who brought him into existence; he is contingent but it is in God that he lives and moves and has his being. This is the realism of the Bible account. Man is a creature, nothing more; but he is a child of God, and he is called to be an heir of God.

Closely allied to what we have just said is the Biblical word on "the image of God." God created man in his own image; God is man's closest relative. Within certain limits—man is created "little lower than God," the Psalmist says—man is like God. How is he like God? The likeness certainly has nothing to do with physical structure; it surely has nothing to do with race or nationality. If man is in the image of God, how is he in the image of God? How is he like God? Well what is God like? He is spirit, person, intelligence; He has creative powers, moral judgment, self-consciousness. Perhaps we can put it this way: since our image has nothing to do with bodily structure or physical characteristics, then it must have to do with those powers which we possess which are non-physical, the powers of the mind and spirit. We too, whatever else we are, are inbreathed with the breath of God; we are living souls; "he has written eternity in our hearts." We too have intelligence, self-consciousness, creative powers and moral judgment, and much more because every man can write his own list. But keep in mind what constitutes the right kind of list. We are in the image of God in those areas of life which we call the things of the spirit, and we are in the image of God when the things of the spirit are under the control of God's Spirit. This introduces another idea which is much on the minds and in the works of scholars today who seek to plumb the depths of this whole concept of the image of God: this image, properly thought about, is always in relationship. If it is in relationship with evil the image is marred; if it is in relationship to God, the image is restored. Here is a kind of brief description of being lost and being saved; the image of God is not only a series of qualities in our lives akin to the qualities in God's life, but these qualities are always being restored in their daily living rela-

[54]

tionship to the Creator God. The image of God is a dynamic not a static reality. God images Himself in us and this is our life which is life indeed.

One other question concerning man's nature remains, a question which puzzled the philosophers first and then the psychologists, a question raised by this whole concept of the image of God (remember, we have just described this as having to do with the things of the spirit) but a question aggravated by the further facts in the creation story that man is not only "inbreathed with the breath of God" but also made of the dust of the earth. He has spiritual qualities but also some very elemental physical stuff. The perennial question has been whether man should be thought of as a body having a spirit or mind or soul, or whether man was to be thought of as a spirit having a body. Close analysis always seems to show that man is at least body and something other than body, of the earth earthy and yet something to be described in terms of mind or spirit. Many thinkers have tried to make man either spirit or body because the problem of making him both mind and body seemed impossible of analysis or definition (cf. our discussion on the Trinity).

Within the last century we have seen this kind of thinking working its way out. Behaviorism developed as a psychology in which man was thought of as only body. He is a thinking body, of course; but his thoughts are only issues of the body—"the mind secretes thought as the liver secretes bile." It was declared by some of

[55]

the enthusiasts that any youngsters rightly conditioned, subjected to the proper stimuli, could be developed in any direction desired. Every action is followed by an equal and opposite reaction—so the physical law goes—therefore act rightly on the body and get the reaction you want. There are buttons to push, wires to pull, and the results can be controlled and so predicted.

It so happens that there is much truth in all this, and the truth tempts us to generalize beyond the facts. Indeed there is so much truth that the engineers of propaganda have learned a great deal about bringing masses of men under control. We still count on considerable "conditioning" in much of what we should prefer to call "leadership." Aldous Huxley in his *Brave New World* about twenty years ago carried this idea to what was then thought to be ridiculous extremes; we wonder now just how close he came to being prophetic. But he was wise enough to have his story hinge on one man, who even in such a perfect system of control could not be perfectly controlled. This man wanted to be free to love which meant for him, within the system, the freedom to suffer. So he chose to love and to suffer and refused all efforts to be brought under complete control. Man is a body; that is self-evident. But he is more than a body; this is his glory and can be his pain.

Instead of saying that man *is* a body we can bring out the opposite emphasis by saying that he *has* a body.

The essential man is not his body; the body is merely housing for the man himself. The Hindus apparently can accept the body as illusion, and the movement called Christian Science has something of this same idea. But generally it has been difficult for Western man to think of the physical as being illusory. There is truth here, nevertheless. The whole idea of the "image of God" gives first place to the things of the spirit in man, in the highest religions there is always the urging that we control the body by the spirit; all forms of self-discipline are the recognition that the higher levels of life are in the mind and spirit and that a man must keep his body under. Some theories of immortality are based on the belief that the body, which is subject to constant change and final decay, is sluffed off and that forever. Immortal life in such thinking becomes the life of disembodied spirits.

The Bible revelation of the nature of man is given its foundation in the second chapter of Genesis. Here the language is simple and universal: that is, not scientific nor technical. But the position is quite clear. Man is a special kind of creature: not spirit and not body, but both at the same time. The body is described as being made of the dust of the earth, out of the elements, as we would say it now; and this body is "inbreathed" with the breath of life. Man is akin to the earth, akin to the lower creation. He is dust and to the dust he returns. At the same time he is of the spirit of God himself. As man he is *both* soul *and* body, and the "inbreathing" of God seems to mean that every cell of his physical being is thus inbreathed. Electric current and the wire which conveys it are not the same thing, not even the same kind of thing, and yet you cannot touch the wire without being shocked by its "life," so is the life of God in man; you cannot touch his body at any point where you do not find him inspirited.

Pascal has commented on this also:

Who would not think, seeing us compose all things of mind and body, but that this mixture would be quite intelligible to us? Yet it is the very thing we least understand. Man is to himself the most wonderful object in nature; for he cannot conceive what the body is, still less what the mind is, *and least of all how a body should be united to a mind*. This is the consummation of his difficulties, and yet *it is his very being*.[3]

All of this then and surely much more, is what we can say about man. Viewed in all the "realism" of the Biblical account there are so many things which can be said of him, said of him alone, not because he is not related to all things in heaven and earth, but because in his own structure there has been created this amazing and delicate balance of all his sources and resources. He is a creature of God, but also a creature of God in the image of God, but even more an image of God which requires a constant relationship of fellowship with God. The image of God is understood in

---

[3] *Ibid.*, p. 21 (italics added for emphasis.)

spiritual qualities and spiritual relationships, yet man is also a physical creature. At the same time every atom of his elemental stuff is "inbreathed" with the breath of God, and he is a living soul, but not in the sense that his body contains that soul but in a more wonderful way; his soul permeates his body. This delicate body-spirit relationship, in constant communion with his Maker: this is man. Who but God could have conceived of such an amazing creature, wrought out his "inner parts," dreamed of his destiny?

All this about man is introduced to our thinking by the end of the second chapter of the Bible! This is the short short story; only two chapters in Genesis. Then something desperate enters into the story—the relationship to God the Creator, the image of God, the relationship among men, the "dominion over the creatures," the controls of spirit over body, the delicate spirit-body harmony—all these are perverted. Here is a darker, starker realism. Sin has entered into life; Sin the destroyer, the perverter, the nasty twist at the heart of things. From the third chapter of Genesis even until now, sin creates the "plot" of the story. What can an Almighty God do to rescue his "lost" creation and restore man to the family of God?

Chapter Five

THE NATURE OF SIN

THE FIRST THREE CHAPTERS OF GENESIS TELL OF THE
creation of the world, the creation of man, and the beginnings of sin. Although written in simple and popular language—and they need to be because of the
universal mission of the Bible—they are nevertheless
profound and true. Their simplicity is not simple-
mindedness and it has been part of the simple-minded-
ness of our day to make such a confusion. The second
chapter of Genesis is the basis for our understanding
of man; the third chapter is basis for our understanding
of sin.

In thinking about man and his nature we tried in the
last of our studies to make clear that man is a creature
of God and therefore a dependent and contingent
being, constantly related to God not only for his creation in the first place but also for his moment-by-
moment existence. Further, he is a creature made in the
likeness of God and created to have fellowship with

God. Finally it is clear from the Genesis description that he is neither a beast nor a god, but a man, a special kind of creation delicately balanced in a unique combination of the "dust of the earth" and the "breath of God." This special creation is open to the onslaughts of sin and is attacked by sin. The attack and man's defeat are described for us in the third chapter of Genesis.

The attack of sin destroys man in his essential nature, at those very points where he is most man. In the first place the image of God in man is marred, not utterly destroyed, but so marred as to be hardly recognizable and now beyond the power of self-healing. In the second place essential creaturehood is destroyed because, having capitulated to the temptation "ye shall be as gods," man now tries to run his own life as if the life were his own, free somehow from the direction and support of God. In the third place sin destroys the fine balance of man's nature—dust of the earth, God-breathed; man now swings back and forth between life on the brute level and life on the god level. In either direction he perverts what he ought to be, and so perverts all his efforts and so perverts his social relationships in this constant and abortive effort to be what he is not. In all these areas he is now in rebellion against his Maker and is at the same time at war with himself and with his neighbor. "Whence come wars and fightings; come they not from the lusts that war within us?"

In casting about for the best way to get at this whole problem of sin I have concluded that the way most helpful to our understanding is to follow the steps in the temptation and fall as they are lined up for us verse by verse and step by step in the third chapter of Genesis. We can see clearly here (and again, do not be fooled by the simplicity of the language and the simplicity of the story) how man, as man, i.e., our first parents, fell, but we see something else; in a very surprising manner we discover that as we follow the temptation and fall of man, we are describing our own temptations and fall. This story about Man is the story about Everyman; the story is so terribly familiar. Our familiarity, I suppose, supports what Scripture teaches us about our personal identity in the Fall. We were there!

We can justify the description of at least ten separate steps in temptation and fall.

1. Eve's attention is drawn to the tempter and she is willing to listen to what he has to say. We have no way of knowing how long the temptation lasts at this point. Was Eve finally worn down, as C. S. Lewis suggests in his re-creation of this event in his *Perelandra?* In any case she finally succumbs to that dangerous point where she listens to what the tempter has to say. She takes the long chance of entering into a conversation with evil. This is showing more confidence in herself than she has any reason to. Instead of fleeing temptation and the tempter she enters into an argument about what sin really is and what it is likely to do to her. Like us she wants to be "big about it all,"

to show her maturity by at least "giving the devil his due." Thinking ourselves to be strong we think we can afford to be tolerant and give good ear to the counter claims of evil as against the will of God. Like Eve, we all show the same kind of false confidence and at the same point and with the same inherent dangers.

2. The tempter raises a question against God and even against the goodness of God. The words "hath God said?" have a sneer in them. How could God really say such a thing? What kind of a god would make a demand like that? Is God keeping something from you that you ought to have, something that is really good for you in the long run?

3. Eve follows this lead and follows it too far. She answers him that God has forbidden them to eat of the fruit; he has also commanded, "Neither shall ye touch it." As far as the record goes, at least, God did not forbid the touching, just the eating. A certain petulance seems to have entered into Eve's side of the conversation as she ponders the idea that maybe God is holding something back. Have you not had a like experience in dealing with children? For their good you withhold some one thing from them to which they often unfairly react, "You don't let us have anything." This, of course, is not true, but is indicative of an attitude toward your commands, a suspicion that what you give and what you withhold may be motivated by something less than your love for them. So with Eve. She has given herself

to the enemy now at least to this extent: God is under suspicion for putting any limits at all on Paradise.

4. The tempter now raises a question not only against the goodness of God but also against the honesty of God. "Ye shall not surely die." This is true and it is not true; it is thus a half-truth. Adam and Eve do not die when they eat the forbidden fruit, at least not in the sense that physical life immediately ceases. At the same time this is true: some wonderful potentialities in them and their environment do die, and physical death is assured them in the end. Here is one of the truly alarming subtleties of sin—its timing. We are able to experiment with sin and even to continue in sin because there is no immediate pay-off in the wages of sin. But the wages are paid, every dime. The half-truth that death is not the wages of sin is Satan's finest tool. In this as in everything else, he is the prince of liars.

5. The next appeal is to wisdom and sophistication. "Your eyes will be opened." Now we can be "in the know." But we already know because God has told us, and God speaks the truth. This is all we need to know. Not so apparently. We must now know by our own personal experience and judgment and not by the word of God. It is this appeal to sophistication which is the trap for so many of us, especially young people. We must experiment with sin for fear we are somehow missing something. Missing what? The destroyer! We seem to sense this in something like the use of dope where the reaction time is brief and destructiveness is

[64]

immediately evident. But here the "timing" gets interlocked with our problem, when, in so many cases we can enjoy the taste of sin, its air of sophisticated intelligence (and pride!) and really find "nothing too harmful." Here is the temptation of our knowledge as against God's knowledge, e.g., sophistication as against wisdom. God knows us, He knows what sin is, He knows what sin will do to us; thus His most solemn warnings. When man sins anyway, there is no going back to live as if the sin had not been committed. We can never say of any event after it has passed that it never really happened. It is like the breaking of a beautiful vase, or the marring of a work of art; we can never pretend that things are just the same again. The steps cannot be retraced exactly, the atonement made is never somehow complete, the reconstruction never looks quite like the original.

6. This next step follows immediately; Eve passes her judgment now according to her sophisticated attitude and not according to God's command. Quite evident to her is the fact that the fruit is "good for food . . . a delight to the eyes . . . desired to make one wise." All these things are indeed true about the fruit—and all are at this point irrelevant. Many things look good in and of themselves. Still stands the command; we are not to eat. The first question is not one of our own argument, whether we can see, as Eve rightly sees, that these things are good in and of themselves; the question is whether there may be some other things about

[65]

sin that we can't know just by simple observation and our own sophisticated judgment. Some things may be good, but not good when taken in disobedience, or mixed with other things, or as contributions to our pride in our own sophistication. Sodium and water are both good, *per se*. But don't mix unless you are perfectly shielded against the destruction of your superficial and ignorant observations. What God knows, and what we are guessing about reality apart from the wisdom of God, may well be at many points two entirely different structures of information. Many sins which go down sweet as honey leave their awful and bitter after-taste. Here again is the subtlety of sin.

7. We are ready and more than ready now for the overt act. Temptation has now led to sin. Temptation and sin are not the same thing, but temptation "played along with" already has sin in it and it is a nice question, many times, as it is in this Genesis account, just where one becomes the other. Potentially, at least, Eve has been on the skids ever since she began believing anything the tempter had to say. Having given her mind and will she now finds no problem in the act. There are plenty of ways of going to Hell and they are all easy; the way is broad. As C. S. Lewis has suggested, the devil doesn't care how fast we go to hell just so long as he can keep us moving in the wrong direction.

8. Having sinned herself, Eve now wants to share her sin; she shares with Adam. Misery loves company and so does sin, perhaps sin more than misery because

we have a special subtle temptation here, the kind of ridiculous belief—and it is very widespread—that if everyone is 'in on the act," then somehow God can't condemn everybody. We have the notion, from where I don't know, that we can lessen our own guilt by sharing it with someone else. It doesn't work. "The soul that sinneth shall surely die."

9. Now our first parents hide themselves from each other and run away to hide themselves from God. Here are the great separations. We recall that man as man was made for fellowship; that fellowship, toward God, toward man, is now destroyed. The idea of "nakedness" is not merely, and I think not chiefly, a question of "nudity" at all. Apart from the twists of our minds and the lusts that entangle us, nakedness is no problem at all, as any artist or surgeon can attest. But how easily it can become a leering, sniggering sort of thing. Here certainly is what spirit can and cannot do to body, inside and outside of sin. All this sort of thing, and much more besides, we all understand too well. But it is my opinion that the emphasis here is more profound. Sin makes our first parents cover themselves up. They clothe their nakedness because they cannot now endure (because of sin) to stand revealed fully to one another. They have pulled down the blinds and they have covered themselves up. Even great friendship and great love, with mutual concern to be completely self-revealing, never quite solves the problem raised by sin here. We talk much today about the

therapy of finding acceptance, or the therapy of having our hidden sins brought to the surface and there released by the comfortable words of a psychiatrist. Of all of this one must say, "Not quite, please, not quite enough." The deeps of our problems are the deeps of sin. Until God, from whom men now flee, find us, as God found man at the beginning, in judgment first, then in promise, then in mighty redemptive acts, then in new birth; unless all of that, we shall hardly heal the hurt.

10. So God comes seeking them out and they tell Him funny little lies, and dream up clever little justifications, and set about to lay the blame on somebody else, even on God. God cuts through all this conversation; the conversation is nothing like the "interesting discussion" they were having on the pros and cons of evil. They were going to be sophisticated because Satan was going to let them "know what the score is." So God tells them what the score is. And henceforth the game will be played outside the garden, on a rough field, and the opponents will not be entirely restrained from dirty play.[4]

How did it all happen; what is the clue to all this?

[4] (Lest I seem somewhat naïve in basing all this discussion on Genesis 3 may I refer you to Milton and his *Paradise Lost* and to books on *Paradise Lost* by C. S. Lewis and Arnold Stein and T. S. Eliot. Other first rate minds besides Milton have also been enthralled by the amazing profundity of this description of temptation and fall. Try Paul, Augustine, Luther, Calvin, Pascal, Wesley, Aquinas, and Reinhold Niebuhr. You haven't begun to think seriously unless you have thought profoundly on Genesis 3.)

In my judgment, the center of the temptation is in this appeal to pride: "ye shall be as gods." As dependent creatures of God we believe that we can move over, even in God's own universe, and even using the life He gives us and sustains in us, to some place where we can operate our lives on our own powers and our own intelligence apart from His will and His way. We know that we need God for our very existence, and we hope in His grace and salvation. Still, we want to run our own lives. We shall decide what is good and what is evil ("ye shall be as gods, knowing good from evil"); we shall obey self rather than God. Maybe we can be good enough to get by. We shall serve God only as it suits us (suits *us* and therefore not necessarily God). We shall discover some way of serving God while still serving the customs and habits of our own community and time. Self now reigns where God should reign; at the same time we are dependent absolutely on the reign of God in providence and care. Without Him and His constant sustaining care we have neither the power nor the place to take our stand even while we act out our rebellion against Him.

Thus life now gets two centers of operation: the necessary one which God has in His care and common grace, and the impossible one of the self where we try to run our own lives over against God. There is now no integration (integer means just one) but disintegration; there is no harmony, for harmony takes a single core for cohesiveness. With two drivers at the controls the machine literally is pulled to pieces. "You *cannot* serve God and mammon," Jesus makes plain to us on the Sermon on the Mount. Or in another way, "If thine eye be single thy whole body shall be full of light; if thine eye be evil thy whole body shall be full of darkness." The opposite of the single eye, the single loyalty, is not double loyalty—even to attempt that is impossible really. The opposite of singleness is not doubleness but "evil," and so our whole body is filled with darkness. Salvation for mankind, whether individual or social, demands integration and so harmony. This means, in this context certainly, that we must have the integration of a single loyalty whether within, in the body politic, or world-wide. Paul hints of it, "It is no longer I that live but Christ liveth in me,". . . "For me to live is Christ." Only thus can we have harmony and peace and strength, return to our right minds free of the confusions and divisions that create insanity, and come back to our essential natures which image God. There must be single and complete commitment. In rebellion against God and with disharmony without and disintegration within, mankind is really cast "out of the garden." How can we enter again through that flame which burns away all dross? That flame demands purity, and Kierkegaard suggests that to be pure is "to will one thing." There is no place in Paradise apparently for double-mindedness, divided loyalties, half-way commitment, some bland blend of our own concoction.

The remainder of Scripture tells us a great many things about this sin of our first parents. One thing is made perfectly clear: what happened to man in Adam happened to man as such. "In Adam all died." Thus now all men are "born in sin." Our sin, as thus construed, does not consist primarily in sinful acts but in our sinful condition of which these acts are manifold and variant symptoms. The Bible is not so much concerned with *sins* as with *sin,* a condition of the whole person who is lost in his rebellion and disobedience, the constant and futile attempt to run his own life against the will of God. The whole person is *lost* in such a condition, he is incapable of returning to God until God acts in a saving way, he is under the guilt of his condition, he suffers the miseries of his inner disintegrations, and he continues to think that by doing the same sort of things harder and more sincerely he shall somehow save himself. He is *dead* wrong!

To describe man's condition theologians have developed two terms: "total depravity" and "original sin." These expressions are not exactly the way they sound. Original Sin does not mean, as I once thought, that there is anything "original" about sin or the way I happen to sin. Sin is a very old and in the last analysis a very routine sort of thing. Our sins are no more original than those of Jezebel or the Borgias. What original sin means is that our life is sinful in its *origins*. We come into the world already tainted, discolored, misdirected. We are hurled into life like a ball with a spin on it and in time the curve "breaks." Original sin means that our origins go all the way back to the very origin, Adam. By virtue of the fact that we are human at all, we participate in the race of which he is head. Human nature is sinful nature and I participate in that nature. Original sin also means that every act of mine has sin in its origins; I cannot do a completely sinless act. Even in my best deeds and my best thoughts there is still the discoloration of self-centeredness instead of God-centeredness. This may easily be illustrated in my pride in my own acts or in my insistence that one of my "good" acts should be given more respect or gratitude.

The expression "total depravity" does not mean that I am totally depraved in the sense of being a madman. (Recent horrors of war would indicate, however, that men are more depraved than we like to think.) But the emphasis is on the word "total." This is a way of saying that the *totality* of my being is touched with the depravity of sin. If sin were blue in color I would be some shade of blue all over. My body is really a body "of death," because, if left to its own tendencies apart from the saving grace of God, there is nothing but death in me—death which is physical, mental, spiritual—total!

The doctrine of sin emphasizes that the race of mankind is a fallen race. As participants in that race, therefore, we are participants in that fallen condition. This fallen condition can be described in such terms as "original sin" and "total depravity" or any other terms which will make clear to us that in and of ourselves there is no good in us that will grow naturally into our own salvation. Only by the regenerative act of God— new birth, a new creation—can a new process be started to restore us to our true and essential humanity, the image of God. The way of this regeneration is established for us in Christ's complete obedience all the way to the cross. The application of this regeneration is only by the power of the Holy Spirit.

Chapter Six

THE PERSON AND WORK OF CHRIST

THE STORY OF THE BIBLE IS THE STORY OF REDEMPTION. When, according to the account in the third chapter of Genesis, man had fallen, God set out to accomplish salvation. We read that He came seeking those who had sinned, He initiated and carried through the action by which they should be found, He pronounced judgment and penalty on their sin. But He also came in Promise, for the third chapter of Genesis (3:15) contains the first promise of Scripture which has come to be known as the Prot-Evangel. The promise tells of the "seed" of woman who shall bruise the head of the serpent. The rest of the Bible story centers on the problem of sin and a series of mighty acts by which God restores men to a saved relationship to Him. God came in the law, in the messages of the prophets, in the holy history of Israel; in the "last days" He came to us in his Son. The Lord Jesus Christ came finally to accomplish redemption.

One enters on the subject of Jesus Christ, especially in a study as brief as this, with considerable hesitation. The words of Horace Bushnell in his *Nature and the Supernatural* are fitting here: "Who can satisfy himself with anything he can say concerning Jesus Christ?" One is surely never satisfied with what he does say, but the *attempt* to learn and to say—surely one can be happily satisfied with the attempt. We are, after all, called to be disciples—learners—and we can continue the satisfying pursuit of learning about him and telling about him to others.

We can begin to "get at" the subject of Jesus Christ by returning to our first remarks about the "mighty acts" of God. The redeeming act of Jesus is in itself a series of "mighty acts." There was first of all the mighty act of *preparation* from all eternity. "The Lamb was slain from the foundation of the world." As nearly as we can contemplate eternal acts and attempt to understand them in the limitations of our temporal language and concepts, God wanted in man, not a creature of innocence, but a creature of virtue; not a process but a person; a creature really wonderful who could, in the image of God, commune with God. He therefore had to give man a choice—for right over wrong; the choice could go desperately wrong and it did. But God, in infinite resource, and we shall see also at what infinite cost, arranged even for this; the Lamb was already provided, ready, freely offered, sufficient. When sin would abound grace would even more abound, and thus every preparation was made to redeem the situation and to save mankind from the consequences of sin.

A second mighty act followed in what we call the *"Incarnation."* This word means "in-fleshed" and defines the fact that God came in the flesh as Christ; or, again that we see in Jesus Christ God Incarnate. Although Christ was born fully man, "born of a woman, born under the law," he was also fully God. Thus in his birth there had to be the mighty act by which he was conceived by the Holy Spirit. (The manner of the birth of Christ, termed the Virgin Birth, might better be defined as the Virgin Conception, for the birth itself was normal enough once he was conceived by the Holy Spirit.) What is demanded in this mighty act of incarnation, however, is that Jesus Christ, born of the Virgin Mary, must be both God and man, born of God, born of a woman; at the same time, in the face of what we have said of original sin and total depravity, the miraculous act of his conception must be such that even in the taking on of full humanity he must be kept clear and clean of the taint of that sin which runs through all those born of natural generation. Here is a good place to remind ourselves that essential humanity *is* sinless, fallen man is sinful: Christ takes on himself human nature without sin.

Jesus of Nazareth, the humanity; Christ, the

anointed one, the deity: thus Jesus Christ is described to us as fully man and fully God. The church has wrestled strenuously to hold these two truths simultaneously and the church has wrestled with equal desperation to get this sort of thing defined. The history of the early church was marked by what we call the Christological controversies, and these in turn were closely related to the Trinitarian controversies. What we say about the two natures and one person in Jesus Christ is closely knit with what we are saying about one God and three persons. The difficulty is the same kind of difficulty that we faced in our chapter on the Trinity: How can two things that are not the same things or even necessarily the same sort of things, be one thing? Enough has been said (cf. chapter 2) to show the extent and limitations of definitions through the help of our illustrations and analogies. We turn aside on this kind of question again here to show that the question of the nature of God, the question of the person of Christ, and indeed, the make-up of our own selves is always the same kind of *question*. If we can accept it or grasp it or define it at the level of the Trinity or in the Person of Christ, or in the analysis of self, we have at that level the clue to the mystery at the other levels. As we once insisted in our discussion of the Trinity, this mystery is the essential mystery of Being, and we find it first or last, as either clue or basic mystery, in the nature of God himself.

Accepting the essential mystery, the church, however, was insistent on the revealed facts. They held eventually, and this has become the core truth in all evangelical churches since, that in Jesus Christ we have just one person and that this one person has two natures, and that these two natures are full and complete —fully God and fully man. Accepting the one person and the two natures we are then directed not to divide the person nor to confuse the natures. And right about there is where we have to leave the problem as far as definition and description are concerned. But note something strange here. We should expect that some such combination as God and man in one person would have to be a kind of monstrosity after the fashion of the inventions of the Greeks, a combination of a man and a horse, for example. In the case of Jesus Christ this is simply not so, not even hinted at, clearly impossible. The gospel accounts describe this Jesus Christ on the stage of history, among ordinary people, in the normal flow of contemporary events. Meanwhile the gospel writers are claiming his deity and his humanity and Jesus is making the same claims. But note this also: he moves as one person with one center of his own self-consciousness and is looked upon by others as just one person. Not only is this single person claiming deity and humanity for himself, and being so described by others, walking his hour upon the stage in perfect naturalness, but increasingly he comes before us as the most attractive person in history, the one we should most like to be. But even more wonderful than this: if you want to know what God is like you find yourself looking at Jesus Christ and *at the same time* and *in the same person* you are looking at Jesus Christ to see what man is like, or what man ought to be like. And be amazed at this also: in four gospels which can be read in their entirety in about eight hours, simple, untrained men, without speculation or philosophizing, in perfect "artlessness" set all this before us. It is the mark of great literature that the characters unfold in real situations and that the plot progresses in the real nature of the people and the situations. Where did Matthew, Mark, Luke and John, with the help, it is suggested of Peter and Paul, dream up a character like Jesus Christ and invent a story in which such a character should unfold? The "artlessness" by which this comes to pass is profound proof of the reality of the figure who steps forward from the pages of the gospels and the profound proof of the inspiration of the writers. Jesus Christ, fully God and fully man, one person, and we must not confuse the natures nor divide the person—all this is plain theological definition—and all this having been said and truly, we still know the wonder and the warmth of this most attractive figure set forth in the Gospels. "Who can satisfy himself with anything he can say concerning Jesus Christ?"

A question closely allied to these questions of the Incarnation has to do with the way in which Jesus was in some fashion limited to humanity while still being fully God. Paul sets the question before us in his letter to the Philippians in the famous "kenosis" (emptying) passage of the second chapter. "He *emptied* himself, taking on the form of a servant, becoming obedient even unto death. . . ." The literature of theologians has abounded in discussions of just how this Jesus Christ could be fully God and yet be subjected to the routines of human life, with necessary limitations thus set upon his deity. Was Jesus really cold and hungry and tired? Were there some things he didn't really know or only half know? How *could* he empty himself?

What I have to say, in the preface of libraries of discussion, is in no way complete, but is an attempt to be helpful in the sense that what I say may be a means of our coming to an understanding of other areas of truth about Jesus. I have always been guided here by what A. H. Strong, the great Baptist theologian said in his *Systematic Theology*. Writing on this *kenosis* (emptying) he said that in this self-abnegation Jesus did not lay aside his divine powers which would have been plainly impossible if he was to remain in any sense deity, but he did lay aside "the independent exercise" of his divine powers. Being on an equality with God was not a thing to be grasped (held on to at all costs) and so for the sake of men and their redemption he emptied himself by laying aside, not the powers, but the right to use them independently. He must do what man has failed to do; he must obey God in human flesh. He must, therefore, seek the will of God, wait for the power of God, be obedient even unto death. He never lost the powers; he gave up, we repeat, their "*independent* exercise." Note for example, and briefly, the temptations of Jesus. The writer to the Hebrews says that Jesus was "tempted in all points like as we are." But I myself am never tempted to turn stones to bread or launch a campaign for my ministry by diving off the pinnacle of the temple, assuming I could climb it in the first place. How then is Jesus tempted as I am tempted? He is tempted to use his powers (as I am tempted to use such powers as I have) in some selfish manner, apart from the will of God, apart from the word of God. Notice that Jesus has the power. He can turn stones to bread and he can cast himself off the pinnacle of the temple. To do so, however, is to destroy what he came to do redemptively. If he is able to "throw his weight around," then he will have advantage in his human experience which we do not have. To that extent and in that way he will not fulfill all righteousness in the flesh as humanity had not been able to before. His victories must be human victories over human temptations. To do this he lays aside the independent exercise of powers he has never in any sense lost.

One illustration may help us. When a man plays with his boy and is hoping to train him, in baseball for example, while he is playing with him, he will have to play with the boy on the boy's level. He will throw at the speed and at the distance the boy can manage; he will hit easy grounders, he will run just fast enough to make the play interesting. In doing all this he will lose none of his own powers. While involved in the game with his boy he can think of his wife, make up his mind about a business deal, turn aside to answer the phone call from another adult, or perhaps protect the boy from a dog or a bully by reasserting his full powers. For the sake of the boy and the boy's situation, however, he "empties" himself of his full powers, which powers he never really loses. Jesus in his prayer conversing with the Father, Jesus at the Transfiguration, Jesus forgiving sins, Jesus laying claim to the "legions of angels" which could be called in for help—there are many hints in the gospels that the powers are all still there. But for our sakes and our redemption, for the sake of the "game," he practiced the great condescension.

Thus we see the "mighty act" of God by which the God-Man entered into history. He had to leave the wonders and powers of his heavenly life to come to live among men; and he had to come to live among men so as to be subject to their laws, worn by their problems, and tempted and tried in all points as are men—yet without sin. His Incarnation was part of his redemptive task, for he had to live now as a man, in perfect obedience, fulfilling the laws of God, as humanity starting with Adam had never been able to do. He had to defeat sin "in the flesh."

There followed other "mighty acts." "Christ's whole life after the Incarnation act is a whole series of acts within the Incarnation, a life on the human stage filled with divine content and meaning. I like to think not only of his life but also of his teaching as an act. The wonderful words of Jesus had power, power to enliven, to judge, to heal, to redeem. In a very special sense, words of truth do act. "To whom shall we go?" exclaimed Peter in a moment of clear understanding. "Thou hast the *words* of eternal life." Words of "life!" And there came at the climax the mighty act of his death on the cross. To this we shall give special study in a later chapter, for it is the central act in the redemptive process and stands squarely at the center of our faith.

In the meantime we note the other acts, all related to our redemption. There was the resurrection: God raised him up "in power." The resurrection of Christ is astounding enough in itself but what is almost equally astounding to our normal ways of thinking is the matter-of-factness with which the gospels treat the event. Take the brief account at the close of Mark's brief gospel: on the part of the women we find amazement, flight, trembling, astonishment, and they are finally frightened into silence. As against this the young man in the tomb directs them as follows: ". . . But go, tell his disciples and Peter that he is going before you to Galilee: there you will see him, as he told you." Well, naturally; why, of course; why not?

In the last account of John's gospel we find the resurrected Lord eating fish for breakfast and some fisherman in the crowd, *in the presence of one risen from the dead* who took the trouble to count all the fish and note that the net was not broken. There is a strange normality about all this as if the resurrection of Christ is just what you would expect, come to think of it. "Why is it thought incredible by any of you," says Paul in the presence of Agrippa, "that God raises the dead?" Why indeed! The resurrection had to happen to validate the cross; that tragedy was crying for God's answer in power, and the answer came. Of course the resurrection; it is the next very natural act in the whole redemptive process. "Do not be amazed . . . he is going before you . . . as he told you."

"He ascended into heaven and sitteth on the right hand of God." So we affirm and so we believe—and so we forget. In his state of exaltation he is again in his rightful position, at the right hand of God where he is able to do for us, because he has died for us, what no one else could possibly do; he makes continual intercession for us. We must never think of the persons of the Trinity as against one another and especially when we are trying to understand intercession by Christ for us. It can't possibly be thought about as if the Father God is against us and the Son is for us. Perhaps we need this picture language of two thrones and two people, one pleading to the other in our behalf. But the Bible warns us against making graven images

[84]

and likenesses of any kind. We need pictures like this only if we immediately discard them when the truth is known; the picture must not be substituted for the truth. The Truth we need to know is that all that Christ has done for us in the cross is now standing in the very presence of God; this *Truth* is our intercession; God knows us henceforth in and through the finished work of Christ. His life eternally, among other things I am sure, is at least this, a saving word spoken endlessly in our behalf. It is a great pity to forget the "continual intercession" for us. Life takes on a different quality when we live near to the constant consciousness that our Redeemer is doing that for us *right now*.

There is a final mighty act; He is coming again. It seems to me that the Bible has not made clear to us, the timing and the exact manner of his appearing. But the fact of Christ's return is certainly made plain enough. As he went away so he shall return, and with his coming will be judgment and newness of life. Christ will return, and men will submit to his rule in terrible judgment or in joyful grace. The fact (not the timing) of the Second Advent is a kind of test of our Christian life now. Is our faith such now that we count ourselves among those who would "love his appearing"?

The redemption story finds its climax in Christ. In these last days God has spoken to us in his Son. But the redemption is not just the "mighty act" on the cross; it is the whole *fact* of Christ. His redemption calls for the preparation, incarnation, life, teachings, death, resurrection, ascension, intercession and second coming. He is our Saviour from first to last. In this, as in all things, he is the Alpha and Omega.

Chapter Seven

THE OFFICES OF CHRIST

IT WAS G. K. CHESTERTON'S WISE OBSERVATION THAT
the only way to make a good statue is to throw away
good marble. The observation is no more relevant
than when dealing with a subject as vast as the life
and work of Christ; we can come to some understanding of something by insisting that we can't talk about
everything, at least, not everything at once, or everything within the covers of one book. If we are to
satisfy ourselves with anything we can say of Jesus
Christ we can do so only by the choice of material
and the discipline of discard.

This sounds like an apology for such a brief treatment as this on the work of Christ, but more exactly
it is an explanation of why the church has been under
the necessity of bringing material about Christ under
the control of certain large issues or certain large
areas of his ministry. Traditionally the church has
come finally to control the study of the work of Christ

under a listing of three offices and the church has more or less come to rest on these three offices: Prophet, Priest and King. The work of Christ begins before the foundation of the world, it is a work interpenetrating all creation at this moment—"in Him all things hang together"—and it is a work which is to continue until all things are summed up in Him. There is, of course, therefore no beginning or ending in our study and understanding of Christ. This is the glory of the study. We select three offices, three areas for study, not to believe that what we have thus said exhausts the subject but because so much can be said briefly and clearly under these three headings. We turn, therefore, to a study of Jesus Christ in his three offices—Prophet, Priest and King.

Christ is a Prophet. Generally we think of a prophet as one who foretells the future. There is truth in this but not enough truth, and such an idea is not the most important truth about the prophetic ministry of Christ. As is so frequently said, a prophet is not so much one who foretells as one who forth-tells; a prophet is one who speaks forth for God. In doing so he may foretell the future but he does not need to foretell the future so long as he is speaking forth —forth-telling—the message of God.

It has always helped me to think of the word prophet —pro—and to think of other ways in which this prefix is used. (We recognize at once that this is just a device for making an idea stick, not a sound way of dividing up the word on philological or etymological principles.) When a man is pro-Nazi or pro-Russian the popular usage is that the man is "for" the Nazis or "for" the Russians, and he is usually "for" them not in some incidental way but all the way. A prophet is someone who is "for" someone or something; a Biblical prophet is someone who is "for" God. He is God's man and he is speaking *for* God. He may be described as an agent, a representative, or more strongly as an ambassador. So long as he speaks for God he is an official representative, and the word ambassador is close to the idea; in such a way he is a prophet. In such speaking he may well foretell, but his basic assignment is that he speak officially and authoritatively for the one whom he represents; he speaks for God. In this sense Christ is a prophet.

It is important that we understand just how this speaking for God is done. My own observation of the prophets of the Bible has led me to recognize in their prophetic words these four steps. First, the prophet points to a situation and describes it; second, the prophet appeals for the reform of this situation as he describes from God's viewpoint how this situation stands; third, he warns of what shall come to pass if the situation is not reformed; fourth, and finally, he pronounces the promises of God through the healing of the situation, or even above and beyond and in spite of what is done with the situation. By such an approach we might consider Amos as a prophet who

[89]

points to the situation and warns of judgment, Hosea as a prophet who appeals for the reform of the situation by a return to God, Isaiah as a prophet who lays before his hearers the eternal promises of God in which, regardless of the response of the people, the Messiah shall nevertheless arise and God's will shall reign supreme. A prophet of our day speaking for God in the same pattern could point to a situation such as the liquor consumption in Washington, D.C., urge his hearers to reform this situation, warn people what can happen to a country where more money is spent on liquor than on education in the nation's capital, and announce finally the assurance that come what may, whether through our obedience or rebellion, through our nation or some other nation, the day will nevertheless arise when "every knee shall bow, every tongue confess." In some such fashion prophetic messages are spoken forth. Note that they are always contemporary, therefore relevant, and therefore, frequently, trouble-making. In such a sense Jesus was a prophet.

In one sense Jesus fulfills the prophetic office uniquely, far beyond our suggestions as to what a prophet is or what a prophet does. He not only speaks the "words" of God which as Peter enthusiastically exclaims are "the words of eternal life," he *is* the word of God. "No man ever spake as this man." He it was that spoke "with authority and not as one of the scribes." We have no notion of down-grading these "wonderful words of life." But their authority was undergirded as it was enhanced by the fact that this one who so spoke did his speaking from a life which was a "Living Word." It can be pointed out with complete justification that much of Jesus' teaching can be found in some related form in other world religions and pre-ëminently in the developing Judaism of the Old Testament. Take the great commandment: "thou shalt love the Lord thy God with all thy heart and with all thy soul and with all thy strength and with all thy mind, and thy neighbor as thyself." We glory in that commandment as a summation of the law of Christ. Yet both parts of the commandment are already imbedded in the teaching and the ethic of the Old Testament. People find deep value in the compassion of a Buddha, the burning zeal of a Mohamet, the social grace and graciousness of a Confucius, and we have no quibble on such points as these. That there are values in other religions no one should deny, in spite of the fact that the values in and of themselves may be highly irrelevant to any total judgment on the religion. One point is crystal clear: regardless of comparisons and contrasts, Christianity has what other religions cannot possibly have. Christianity has Christ. Jesus not only teaches love of God and love of neighbor; he not only brings the two parts of the commandment together into one inter-locked and necessary relationship; he not only puts the parts in their proper order: he *lives* the commandment. He is the only one who ever has,

[91]

and he did it from the manger to the cross. Jesus is not only the teacher of imperishable truth; he *is* the Truth. He is the Living Word, his own teachings come alive in himself. He not only tells us to do but he is at the same time the perfect example of what and how to do. And all this is true in an abiding sense; through the ministry of the Holy Spirit we have the abiding presence of Christ in us, and his living word can come alive in us. We become not only messengers but messages, "living epistles known and read of all men."

Christ is Priest, as well as Prophet. Just as Christ has the double function as a prophet of giving us words of life and being at the same time the Living Word, so he has a double function in his office as priest. He not only offers up the sacrifice in his office of priest; he is the very sacrifice which he offers up. He need not go beyond himself to find either the offerer or the offering.

In the Old Testament precursors of the New Testament there was set forth a very complex sacrificial system, a system culminating in the Day of Atonement when the high priest, on this one day of each year, entered the Holy of holies in the tabernacle and later in the temple, and made the sacrifice of atonement for all the people. He stood in the presence of God for those who could not themselves there stand. Sacrifice was made for the people, but before that could be done some things had to be done for the high priest himself. He had to prepare himself to represent the people and he had to prepare himself to stand before God. He prepared himself internally by making sacrifice for his own sins and he prepared himself externally by washing his body and changing his garments. When he then proceeded to make the sacrifice, the animal sacrificed had also to be clean. We understand, of course, that we are talking in all this of ceremonial cleanness, for the priest was clean neither inside nor out, nor was the animal completely without blemish however hand-picked he may have been. Such purity is not of men and beasts. But in Christ we have not only the fulfillment of all which has been pre-typed for us, but we enter into an entirely new order of things. When Jesus fulfills the office of priest he is himself a priest of such purity that he needs no cleansing; he is also the Lamb without blemish who is offered, and here also his purity is absolute and not relative.

We have therefore the priest without sin offering the Lamb without blemish. We must underline that in all such language one thing is perfectly clear; in this case, *Jesus offers himself*. Say it again and clearly: he is the sinless priest and the lamb without blemish and as priest he has no sacrifice to offer but himself. This he does positively and willingly: "He set his face steadfastly to go to Jerusalem," knowing full well that this was the way to Golgotha. He said of himself, "No one taketh my life from me; I lay it down of myself." There was no other good enough as either priest or sacrifice to pay the price for sin; he paid the price, he alone, and he completely, an infinite price for the infinite requirements of God. Satisfaction was complete.

Christ is Prophet and Priest—and King. See now the interesting doubling in this kingly office also. He is the Ruler who nevertheless rules as Servant Lord. Most of our ideas of kingship are either those of an oriental potentate or of a mediaeval king, a man ruling by maneuver or might. Such a one either has or seeks to have absolute power and authority, and his powers constantly tend to create in him a hunger for more power, and thus kingship keeps edging toward tyranny. His office has many external marks of his authority. He wears royal robes; he wears a crown; he carries the scepter; his seal makes final the laws of the land. In terms of kingship, as that office is popularly conceived, Christ has every right, in the highest sense the "divine right," to all the powers and all the marks of power. Because of his nature and position he has all power in heaven and on earth, all authority is given to him, the Father has given all things into his hands, in his exaltation he is "at the right hand of God." He has rights as Creator and as Judge. His word is our law and absolute obedience is required of us because of his crown rights over us. If he should now appear in any earthly place he would have every right to sit on the highest throne, wear the richest garb, demand abject obeisance. We, on our part, would feel under com-

[94]

pulsion to kneel in his presence or even fall flat on our faces. By any standards by which we can picture kingship we find Christ with every right to such kingship—and certainly much more beyond our imaginings. His powers are by right, and are so absolute that there is no kingship in our experience to contain him. He is King of kings and Lord of lords, and that forever and ever. Finally, for our thinking, he breaks the bounds of all other ideas of kingship; eventually it is his kingship which tells us what proper kingship should be.

There is, however, a second side to kingship; and this, it appears from the Scripture record, is more important; at least it is more important for us to understand it, because otherwise we can get false notions of what is exalted and what is base, what is high and what is low. Think of it this way. If we take Lincoln as a king among men, just how would we add to what he is by placing him on a throne or dressing him in a royal robe? Lincoln would be no more important to us and no more demanding of our respect just because we dressed him in a more expensive suit. We would suspect, rather, that any of our efforts to honor Lincoln by bowing in his presence or dressing him in the trappings of royalty would cheapen rather than glorify him. He has no need of what we can give him except insofar as we honor him with our spirit, honor him in trying to be like him, honor him in honoring the things for which he stands.

So it is, only infinitely more, in our honor of Christ. Christ is King and he comes as a king and fulfills the office of a king, but he reigns as suffering servant. Isaiah's description of him, "there was no beauty that one should desire him," is relevant here. The one who works as his Father worked, and works redemptively on our behalf, whose head was sorely wounded, whose body was scourged and made a whipping-post for us and our transgressions, is not one we would want to honor in the same way we would honor some potentate or tyrant strutting and posturing in his own self-centered and contemptible pride. Our Lord and King is revealed in the one who walked the dusty roads of Palestine, who had no place to lay his head, who emptied himself in obedience all the way to the cross. "Let him who is great among you minister."

Note how the footwashing scene is given exaggeration by the way the action is introduced in the Gospel according to John. "Jesus knowing that the Father had given all things into his hands and that he came forth from God and returneth to him again . . ."— here is description of the rights and powers of a king. Now then, what will he do? Climb on a throne? Demand obeisance? Shout orders? What indeed, does he do? He washes feet! No wonder Peter couldn't stand the idea at all. Peter, maker of the great Confession, simply could not stomach having the Christ in the role of a menial servant. Jesus, "knowing that the Father had given all things into his hands . . ."

washed feet! "Blessed is he that findeth no occasion of stumbling (of being scandalized) in me."

One would hardly know whether royal robes and thrones and parades and neon lights could in any sense have anything to do with such a one. He needs no decoration from us. There is nothing we have that we can give him except the homage of our hearts. We can offer *him* something only when we offer *someone else* something, a cup of cold water "to one of the least." He will not despise those who are of "a broken and contrite heart," in some way "the last shall be first and the first last," multitudes of humble heart and hidden walks who never even knew they fed him when they fed the hungry, he will lift up to reign with him and with all his saints forever; but one gets the subtle notion that if we really want to reign with him the way kings usually reign we shall have missed the whole point of his kind of kingship.

We honor Christ the King who rules in authority and might and power, but who rules always in grace and kindness and service. He plainly tells us in his kind of kingship what really is "high and lifted up," and thereby sets in focus all other values human and divine.

Chapter Eight

THE CROSS OF CHRIST

THE STORY OF THE BIBLE, WE SAY AGAIN, IS THE STORY
of redemption. This story, fundamentally, is the history of mankind. Man fell from the estate wherein
he was created and his life ever since has been marked
by sin and sin's consequences. Over against this fallen
condition of man God has acted, and the history of
man shows man's reaction to God's action. The end
of history is determined by God's plan for our salvation showing itself in our acceptance or refusal of
his free and gracious invitation to become citizens of
his eternal Kingdom.

The central act in God's saving plan is the cross of
Jesus Christ. There on the cross of Calvary was
wrought out for mankind the way of salvation, completely, once and for all. Men have been trying ever
since to explain what it was that happened there. That
great transaction on the cross made it possible in some
way for God to save us by grace. What happened there

to God? What happened to Christ? What happened or can happen to humanity because of the cross? The Scripture records are full of verses giving us facets and insights with regard to this great event. Depending on starting place and emphasis, scholars across the years have come forward with a wide variety of explanations.

The starting place is a recognition that man's sin, pride leading to disobedience, has also meant separation. Since God and man are separated, how can they be made "at one" again? The means by which they have been made "at one" is called the Atonement and we are on perfectly solid ground when we see in the structure of this word Atonement the very thing we are trying to say about what took place on the cross. The cross wrought out Atonement; atonement is the "at one"-ment again of God and man. It is because of this word and what it means that we have theories of the Atonement, theories which have been explanations of what took place on the cross. It is our purpose to examine some of these views and viewpoints, all of which, by the way, have some measure of truth in them. But we must say also, and say it now, that no view is sufficient to define all of the rich meaning of that Atonement worked out for us by God in Jesus Christ.

One of the first theories of the Atonement, and one of the earliest, says that the Christ of the Cross serves as our great *Example*. This is certainly true. In three of the four gospels are these words: "If any man would come after me let him deny himself and take up his cross and follow me." In First Peter (2:21) even the word "example" is used: ". . . Christ also suffered for you, leaving you an example that you should follow in his steps." We are to suffer in some fashion as he has suffered; there is no such thing as a crossless Christianity. Jesus is the pre-ëminent example in all things; the "Imitation of Christ" can serve as a program for life. We see clearly, therefore, that the sufferings of Christ, climaxed in the cross, are, and ought to be, examples for his followers. There is truth, therefore, in this viewpoint.

The only trouble with the cross *merely* as "example" is that it is superficial at the very point where we most need help. Example helps the human hurt very little. We are surrounded with examples; we have enough precepts in our copy-books, enough heroes in our story books, to last any man a lifetime or two. To add to this list of examples the matchless example of Christ's courage means nothing more to us than another completely unattainable goal. We need example, but our deepest need is for enabling power. "Who will deliver me from the body of this death?" There is our real problem. The cross of Christ as an example, if it is only an example without providing for the release from sin, can be for us, not good news at all but simply an exquisite way of breaking our hearts. Before we can even begin to live up

[100]

to such an example—and we admit that it is a matchless one—we must be released from sin and guilt and habit and death. Example alone cannot do this sort of thing.

Closely related to the example theory is what Bushnell finally titled the "moral influence theory." The emphasis is again put on the example of Christ's sufferings but with this difference: we are now personally identified with the one who suffers on the cross—what he was doing there he was doing for us. We can see the difference between these two views of the Atonement if we parallel two similar acts of courage. Take a man who has gone out to battle and who has, against great odds and beyond the call of duty, fought to his own death. Meanwhile by his act of courage and devotion he has turned the tide of battle. What a marvelous example this becomes for all succeeding generations of soldiers. But suppose, rather, that in the heat of battle this same man has fought against these same odds and lost his life just as surely, but has done so to rescue me where I have fallen in helplessness on the battlefield. The courage is still the same but there is this tremendous difference: henceforth, for me, there will be the consciousness that what he did he did for me. He gave his life for me; I live because he died. The moral influence of this act will therefore have tremendous bearing on what I do with my life, how I shall live my life. The theory points up a great truth regarding Christ's death. He died for us, and it was not for a righteous or friendly or attractive man that Christ died. He died, the righteous for the unrighteous, the lovely for the unlovely, the sinless for the sinner; he died even for those who were putting him to death. God commends his love to us "in that while we were yet sinners Christ died for us."

The "moral influence" theory has truth but it is superficial. There is no reason really, in man, or in man's history, to believe that when one person dies for another, then the one who receives this gift will therefore and henceforth be a better man. At Westminster College in New Wilmington, Pennsylvania, there stands the McGill Library built by a man named Mack who had a great friend named McGill who was a missionary in Egypt. Missionary McGill lost his life in the Mediterranean Sea near Alexandria helping in the rescue of an Egyptian girl. The loss of Dr. McGill was incalculable; the Egyptian girl lived the days of her years, as far as one may humanly judge, in futility, triviality and shoddiness. A good man in an act of gracious courage laid down his life for her and out of all this, humanly speaking, came nothing! To think of the cross as example or even the moral influence of example is true but not true enough; it tries to solve the problem of human sin without remembering what a subtle, twisted, devilish, tyrannical thing sin is, without remembering that the man who would follow the great example is at the very origin of his first step in following the example, already disabled in his vision of the example and in his will to follow.

Other views of the Atonement have probed deeper. Grotius, a Dutch lawyer, in what is called the Grotian view, sees our sin as the breaking of God's law and the Atonement as an act of Jesus Christ by which he not only fulfills the requirements of the laws of God in a life of perfect obedience but also takes upon himself in the cross itself the penalities inflicted for our breaking of the law. In this sense Grotius is serious about what sin costs, recognizing that satisfaction must be made for the breaking of God's law; he knows that the satisfaction must be over and above the requirements of the law and that therefore we need a substitute who will live out all the requirements of the law (therefore not owing anything himself to the law before he acts for us) and a substitute of such stature that he can in himself bear what humanity can not bear, namely, the penalties of law-breaking.

Grotius gets us nearer to the heart of things. He introduces the ideas of satisfaction and substitution and recognizes fully not only the cost of sin but also how necessary it is that someone else bear this cost. As a lawyer he is not bothered by the fact that someone else pays the price for our sin, that the guiltless stands for the guilty; the only requirement is that the demands of the law be satisfied by someone capable of that satisfaction. Jesus is the one who pays the price, he pays it pre-ëminently on the cross, the law is satisfied, nothing more is required. The very neatness of this theory, in spite of the deeper truths with which it wrestles, is its weakness. The whole solution of Grotius is somehow too legalistic. God keeps the whole problem at arm's length; satisfaction is complete for the law (and such satisfaction is necessary, we admit) but it is hard to see how two persons, God and man, now have "at one"-ment through such an experience. My stealing from you may be "satisfied" by my paying back what I have stolen and even by paying a fine to satisfy the social structure in which we both live and to give me sufficient punishment for my crime. But when these satisfactions are complete will you and I be any closer together? Has there been any atonement? I think not.

Anselm, a mediaeval monk and scholar, although he is earlier in history than Grotius, was closer to the truth than was Grotius in his later treatment. In his *Cur Deus Homo* (Why God Became Man) Anselm was raising the whole question of why we need a God-Man entering into history in the person of Jesus Christ and why such a one was the only possible means of working out the Atonement. His book is one of the great classics in theology. At the center of our discussion here Anselm describes the sin of man as something perpetrated against the honor and majesty of God. This is where he is deeper than Grotius. The law of God, (which was Grotius' problem) is external to God, but what Anselm is talking about as the honor and majesty of God has to do with God's very person.

We can understand this by trying to understand how people in Anselm's day would look on the honor and majesty of a king. Such attributes and powers as honor and majesty have to do with the very person of the king. Thus, in Anselm's language, and allowing for his day, we see that he is making clear to us that our sin is an affront to God himself, not his law but his person. This is an infinite affront and requires an infinite satisfaction.

Anselm reasons, and it is not too difficult to follow him, that the guilt is man's and must be paid by him, but that the price is infinite and can therefore be paid only by God. Only man owes the debt and he cannot pay; only God can pay the debt and he does not owe. Therefore only a God-Man, namely Jesus Christ, can bear the human sin and guilt and at the same time pay the infinite price. This is *Cur Deus Homo;* this is why God became man.

Somewhere, in and around Anselm's solution, we must find our own solution, but in the meantime we must turn aside to one other explanation of the Atonement, one which Aulèn in his *Christus Victor* brought to the attention of the church at the beginning of this century, a view which he looked upon as the "classic" view, a view which had been submerged, as he thought, for centuries because of the ascendancy of the view of Anselm and variations of emphasis on Anselm's view. Aulèn continues to hold such words as "substitution" and "satisfaction" but in a very much weakened sense, as payment, or price, or penalty. When Jesus cries out on the cross "It is finished," his cry is a cry of victory. He is indeed *Christus Victor*. What victory has he won? Just this: as our champion, Christ, by taking on human nature, has entered into the arena of life and fought the forces of evil and fought these forces all the way to the death, even the death on the cross. In the face of testing and temptation Christ defeats sin in the flesh. Fighting this battle for us he is our substitute, if you like; defeating sin in the flesh he is satisfying the demands of God. To this extent he uses the same words but does not have the same basic ideas as Grotius and Anselm. By eliminating punishment and penalty, by muting the very idea of the wrath of God poured out against sin, his same vocabulary serves to give a different view of the Atonement. Once again we must accept the truth of this view—Christ is the captain of our salvation, our file leader, our champion. But does this answer that one other problem: sin is an act *against* God, not just a failure demanding new victory. How does *God* react *against* sin? How does Christ stand between us and that action of God? No theory of the Atonement approaches any fullness— example, moral influence, "classic" or Grotian—unless we have such concepts as satisfaction, substitution, penalty and the like, and in the "classic" view and the Grotian view we have the use, at least, of these concepts. But the use is still incomplete unless we see, as Anselm shows us, that the offense of sin is primarily an offense against Almighty God and that this offense makes infinite demands on the sinner, in some way, to "pay up!"

We return again, therefore, to Anselm. He makes perfectly clear that a price must be paid. But by whom and to whom? Well, the price must be paid *by* Christ, the God-Man. But to whom is it to be paid? For centuries the idea was quite acceptable to great segments of the church that the price was paid to the Devil. This view at least took seriously the idea of the ransom and the price. But as you read the literature on such a view you begin to wonder about the mechanics of the arrangement and indeed the morality of the arrangement. God gave his Son to the Devil, because the Devil possessed us; the Devil then released us because the price was satisfactory. The Devil then awoke to discover in amazement that God's Son could not be held captive by him; so the Son escaped and thus everyone was free. We were free because we were released by the payment of the price, and the Son was free because in his infinite power, he simply could not be held. This seems a fanciful solution to us now until we remember what it was that men were seriously trying to grapple with. It was this whole question of ransom, or price; it was this whole problem of satisfaction. However incomplete our interpretations of the Atonement may be allowed to be, we must never allow them to be so incomplete as to leave out what Scripture teaches. We must not be untrue to the record just because we have remaining problems of interpreting that record. The Bible speaks of ransom, penalty, cost, etc. And if we do not pay this sort of thing to the Devil then we are still faced with the question: who pays whom?

Anselm thinks the payment is made to God. This is the solution with which I am in agreement but with one proviso, although it is a big proviso. Sin is an offense against God and an infinite price is thus demanded. Only Christ can pay that price and he pays it because as God-Man he carries man with him, man who owes the price. All this is clear enough and with all this I can agree once I can resolve Anselm's mediaevalisms into my twentieth-century vocabulary. But my proviso is this: however we try to think and try to express this matter of payment we must never say it and never picture it in such fashion that we throw one part of the Trinity against another part of the Trinity. I find people slipping into the belief that God hates us and Christ loves us, that God is against us and that Christ is for us; the language of the Atonement is used in such a strong way that the first thing we know we have Jesus Christ standing for us against God who is not standing for us. We forget that "God so loved the world," that Jesus demanded clarity at this point: "He that hath seen me hath seen the Father." It is well enough to recognize that handling the Subject of the Trinity we are already in intellectual difficulty, but we must never falsify the truths of the Trinity, (we must not divide the essence) in order to tidy up our description of the plan of salvation. However we may construe the wrath of God or the love of Christ, it cannot be in such fashion that God is not love or that Christ does not himself pass God's own judgment on sin.

Thus far we have been careful to insist on a view of the Atonement that will not evade the issues raised by such words as satisfaction, substitution and penalty, accepting at the same time the secondary insights set before us by Aulèn and Horace Bushnell. Now we are faced with the problem raised by the mechanics of a view like Anselm's, a view with which we have fundamental agreement. What shall we do with this question of making a payment to God, Christ's making a payment to God, the impossibility, from what we understand of the Trinity, for such a payment to be made from one to the other without dividing God himself? The clue, it seems to me, lies in some words of Paul, where he says in writing to the Corinthians (2 Cor. 5:19) "God was in Christ reconciling the world to himself." *God* was *in* Christ. We have known this all along; we must insist on it and emphasize it in understanding the cross. Whatever was happening there, God was there; when we see Christ there we see the Father also. Vocabulary breaks down and our senses reel before the final mystery of the cross, but we make our insistence again in these theological matters: we cannot fail to say what we do know because we are still mystified by what we do not know. When Christ was crucified, God was *in* Christ.

We can therefore say all that we have said—God demanded the full and infinite price, man could not pay and therefore for satisfaction there had to be the substitute, even Jesus Christ who bore our sin and our guilt, paid the price even unto death. But when we say all this we are saying it of God who in love, as in holiness, having demanded the price, paid the price himself, thus satisfying his own demands in both holiness and love.

Two illustrations have always helped me here. The first one is from the writings of the British theologian, P. T. Forsyth. He tells of the revolutionary activities of a man named Shamel who was fighting against the Czarist regime in Russia about 1870. His was a guerilla group, including not only the fighting men but also their families and their livestock, a group hanging together that they might not all hang separately, to recall some of our own early revolutionary tenets. His organization was his own tight little universe, with laws fundamental to its own existence. Then one day stealing broke out in his camp and his organization began to fall apart in mutual suspicion. So Shamel laid down the law and announced the penalty. "Thou shalt not steal," and the penalty was one hundred lashes. Before long the thief was caught. But it was Shamel's own mother! Now he had the problem of law and love. For the sake of his universe the law must stand;

in no society can stealing be treated with indifference. At the same time he loved his mother and could not face the requirements of his own law that she should bear the one hundred lashes. Who could see his own mother bear such a beating? Shamel shut himself in his own tent for three days trying to find his solution and finally came out with his mind made up; his mother, for the sake of the law and for the sake of the whole society must receive the lashes. How many societies have failed because at this very point they could not hold to the law! But before three blows had fallen Shamel had his real and final solution, his revelation. He removed his mother from her penalty and required that they lay on his own back the full measure of every blow. The price had to be paid in full, but the price was paid by him. His law stood; his love stood. The only possible solution was to receive the punishment in his own person. This, in the last analysis, is what cross-bearing must always be: there is no minimizing of the penalty or weakening of the law, but always payment in full; but the cross bearer makes the payment himself and thus becomes a redeemer.

Something close to this had to happen on the Cross of Christ. God's holiness and God's laws which are necessary expressions of his holiness, had to be satisfied. At the same time something else had to be satisfied—God's love, love to the uttermost, a love that will not let us go. Both holiness and love are of the very essence of God, and both must be satisfied. Too many discussions of the Atonement think of satisfaction only in terms of holiness and justice; the satisfactions of love make their infinite demands also. "God was in Christ," so that when Christ died on the cross the holiness of God was satisfied and so was his love; he took the penalty on himself. Only in the cross could anything like this have happened.

With the satisfaction there was also substitution. Christ did for us what we could not do ourselves. "There was no other good enough to pay the price of sin." Christ was this lamb "without blemish," an offering of infinite value for rebellion against an infinite God. No one took His life from him; he laid it down of himself. All this he did because he loved us with an everlasting love. He had to put himself in our place not only to satisfy himself (God) but also to express that love which would not and could not see us lost.

There is reconciliation here also. We are told to come to the foot of the cross and this we should do, not only to see what our sin is, not only to see what God in his love has done for sin, but also to respond to that holiness and love which are exhibited on the Cross. If we return for a moment to our illustration about Shamel and his mother, we can well ask this question: "What will Shamel's mother do henceforth about her stealing?" We may be sure that between her and her next act of sin will always be the vision of the bloody back of the one who suffered in her stead. "With his stripes we are healed." In some sense we become reconciled to God when we see the Cross, when we really see what sin is, what sin does, what God has to do about sin, *when we really see* what He has done for us.

A second illustration helps us with the idea of reconciliation. About fifteen years ago I was sitting at the dining-room table looking out the window and watching five boys "fooling around" with a B-B gun and wondering a little to myself how long it would be before one of them shot another one in the eye. Finally one of them grabbed the gun to shoot at a little sparrow sitting on a tree just outside the dining-room window through which I had been watching this whole performance. I could see the whole action unfolding before my eyes; it seemed almost slow-motion, uncanny, inevitable. The boy aimed deliberately at the bird, shot at the bird, missed the bird and put a hole in the window right in front of me, and away they all ran with me racing out of the house after them. (I didn't catch any of them!)

In a few days I had found out that a boy named Dave White had pulled the trigger. Also in a few days I had the window fixed and paid for. Then I began to think about Dave. He was evading me at every turn. He would not face me and he had no notion of confessing. In the meantime the other boys had floated back to games in the vacant lot and in the street in front of the house, while Dave, the guilty one, was on the outside of all this, "weeping and gnashing his teeth."

He would have none of us. So I went after him, not to punish him but to save him. He had to face me in judgment, then in grace; only thus could we renew our fellowship, only thus could I bring him back to the gang. I became "The Hound of Heaven," and pursued him until I caught him, and caught him alone. Now we stood face to face to have it out. The boy was rebellious, tense, tight, ready to fight me, ready to run away again. He admitted he had wronged me but I gave him the surprising message that the window had been paid for, that I had no notion of collecting anything from him, that what really interested me was to know how we could get him to come back to be one of the gang again. I really was preaching the gospel to him! I told him over and over again the same old story: the price has been paid; it's all over; let's be friends. What a time I had getting that message through to him. Why? Because he didn't *believe* me. There is always an unbelievable quality in the wonder of what we call grace. But I wish you could have seen him when he finally did believe me. What a wonderful look, what a release of tensions, what a rolling away of the burdens, what a newness of life. Now he could quit running. Now he could relax. Talk about peace of mind; you should have seen that boy. What total commitment he offered me henceforth and by no request of mine! There was nothing he wouldn't do for me; for the first time I understood why Paul introduced himself so many times as a "bond-servant" of Jesus Christ. The boy finally believed that he was justified, "declared right"; for the first time in weeks he had peace. "Who hath believed our report?" It is all over; it is paid in full. "God was in Christ reconciling the world to himself." His message to us now is a simple one: "Be ye reconciled."

Satisfaction, substitution, reconciliation—these can be heavy theological words, but they need not be once we understand what they are saying to us. God's holiness and God's love have been satisfied. This has been accomplished in a wonderful way because God Himself in Christ took upon himself the price which we could never have possibly paid. And now comes the reconciliation, God's pleading with us to believe in and accept what he has already done for us once and for all. It is God Almighty who is appealing to us. How can there be hesitance and indifference about such a message?

But there is more. In the miracle of the Incarnation Christ took upon himself what we know as human nature. Such human nature as we have is tortured and discolored with sin. The offer of salvation is that since the way has been opened to salvation through the precious blood of Christ, and since the price has been paid, and since all is in readiness for our new life, there is now actually available for us the kind of redeemed human life which is the very life of Christ.

We are to be united with Him, caught up in His life. There, as if by a great transfusion, "the blood of Christ keeps cleansing us from sin." Justified—declared now to be right—because of what took place on the cross, we are now enabled by His life in ours to do right.

Chapter Nine

UNDERSTANDING THE HOLY
SPIRIT

WITH THE POSSIBLE EXCEPTION OF THE TRINITY, IT IS
more difficult to treat clearly of the Holy Spirit than
of any other truth in our Christian faith. There are
several reasons why this is so. The most obvious reason
is that we are not purely spiritual beings ourselves and
so have difficulty finding parallels and analogies in
our own experience to something or someone who is
pure spirit. It is common to all of us that when we
want to understand something or explain something
to somebody else, we have to find exact words for expression—and words are symbols—or we have to find
parallel symbols in experience with which we can
compare and contrast the objects of our examination.
How can this be done with the Holy Spirit? As soon
as we make him like something, we have to make him
like something in human experience; but since he is

pure Spirit, we cannot enclose him or his nature in anything which we are able to grasp with our five physical senses. The Holy Spirit, therefore, constantly evades, not from *his* nature but from *our* nature, any suitable analysis or definition which will make him clear to us. It is a problem akin to drawing a picture of a soul, or weighing a thought, or giving shape to an emotion. The tools we have do not quite fit our problem.

Another reason we have trouble in grasping the Holy Spirit with our understanding is that the chief office of the Holy Spirit is not so much to reveal truth concerning himself as it is to reveal truth concerning Someone Else. Since he is the Spirit of Truth, then any truth we have concerning him must come from him as the source; but in giving us truth in obedience to the requirements of his office he keeps pointing in that other direction. The Holy Spirit "takes of the things of Christ and shows them unto us." "Over there," he says, "is what you are really looking for, because if I can get you to see Christ I can get you to see God." It is like the experience of looking at the sun; the sun blinds us by its own light because we are not rightly equipped to look at the sun. But in the light of the sun we can look at other things. We know that it is only by that light which we cannot look upon that we are able to look at anything at all.

We know of the Spirit's existence and of his offices and powers, not by an original discovery of him nor by the cleverness of our analysis and definition, but only because the Scriptures, which were inspired by the Spirit and made known to us by the same Spirit, reveal the fact and the nature of the Spirit and his operations. We find the Spirit at work through all the history of the Old Testament and we find him moving into the forefront of activity in the New Testament. The Book of the Acts, the "Acts of the Risen Lord," would be meaningless without the acceptance of the fact of the Holy Spirit and of his work in the early church. It has been the belief of the Church through all its history that the Holy Spirit has continued to be operative in persons and in the life of the Church, and that Church history apart from the work of the Holy Spirit would be without meaning. The history of the Church without the Spirit, if such a history could have even been possible, would have been without power and without life. In contemporary problems, whether personal or ecclesiastical, we continue to pray for the Spirit's guidance and power.

We face then this impasse: the Holy Spirit is clearly set forth in Scripture as one of the persons of the Trinity and as such, a proper object of serious study and reverent adoration. He nevertheless, by his very nature and office, constantly evades our grasp and understanding, especially as we try to share with others what we ourselves have received, more by heart than by head, of his marvelous reality and constant, strengthening comfort. In the face of this dilemma, and realizing the limitations of our analysis, I have found it helpful in my own thinking as well as in my teaching to seek out an analogy, or rather a series of analogies. This approach is, of course, incomplete, as we have discovered by this time in the use of all analogies. The purpose thus served is not so much a description of the Holy Spirit as a revealing of how we believe, in other areas of our experience, in other realities and other powers which are likewise beyond our total comprehension and final definition. Although we do not have symbols in the world of sense experience which will show us what the Holy Spirit is, we do have experiences of other powers in our world which will show us what the Holy Spirit is like.

Every power we know is, in the first place, *indefinable*. We easily forget this. We have a variety of powers channeled through various machines and engines; but power, as such, is beyond our definition. Everyone believes in cause and effect and every effect demands a cause, at least in the usual way we think about things. But when the cause produces the effect, what is the power between the two which makes one thing lead to another. We know that energy apparently moves from one thing into the other thing. But what, by definition, is energy? Or take, for example, a more common "thing" like electricity. Did you know that we still have no definition for electricity? We do not know how electricity flows through a wire; we do not even know what flows through what or even whether it is proper to use the word "flow." We can name the power and measure its speed and amount, and we know how "powerful" it is, but the nature of the thing in itself will not subject itself to definition. Electricity is what *does* the certain things that we have been observing. At the same time, notice that in our use of electricity no one hesitates to talk about it and no one hesitates to use it, just because no one is capable of defining it. We would be greatly impoverished in this modern day if we awaited definition, and certainly if we awaited an easy and popular definition, before we believed in or made use of this marvelous power. It is surprising how many people will not pray for the Spirit, or in the Spirit, until they get a definition. As far as I can tell now there will be no easy popular definition forthcoming.

In the second place power is *invisible*. We can see manifestations of power but we do not see the power itself. I remember how surprised I was to learn in physics that steam is invisible. I thought I had been looking at steam all my days. Not so, the physicists assured me. It is only when steam turns into something else, when it becomes water, that we are able to see, not steam, but what steam becomes; the steam itself is an invisible something, doing its work, then escaping in a form which is now visible. A marine once told me of his first experience with radar and the strange feeling it gave him. He was invited aboard a destroyer tied up in the Hudson River and there had his first experience with something which we use in all kinds of ways now but which was entirely new to him then. In simplicity it was described in this way. A unit of energy was sent out into space and it bounced back again. Something invisible had gone out—there had certainly been a *real* thing; call it a unit of energy if you like—and the thing bounced back, registering the time of its trip out and back, and so registering the distance of the trip it took, and registering furthermore that there was something else "out there" which the unit of energy had hit and from which it had returned. Measuring the time it took for the unit of energy to go out and back and turning the time measurements into space measurements, the radar operators were able to tell how far away the thing "out there" had to be. They sent out an inquiring message and received a definite answer—and no one saw anything! We take this sort of thing so much for granted now that it is worth thinking about once again in its simplicity before we forget what is really happening. Now we can bounce these units of energy off the moon, or use them for discovering speeding rockets or lurking submarines. Our indefinable, invisible units of energy have become basic essentials in national defense. Meanwhile these "realities" of such basic importance are still beyond our five senses and beyond our definitions.

In the third place power is *inviolable*. Power always operates according to its own nature and follows its own laws. We sometimes think we are using electricity, and in a sense we do, but never by making electricity obey our wills. Rather we have to discover the nature and laws of electricity first and use the power according to its own inner essence. "The wind bloweth where it listeth . . . so is the Spirit of God." Thus in simple analogy Jesus described the operations of the Holy Spirit in terms of the wind, which also is beyond definition, which also is invisible, which is indeed inviolable. Men who would sail the seas must discover how to use the wind, build their crafts in obedience to the wind, run before it, or tack into it, or even get out of it entirely. The wind bloweth where it listeth and can becalm us or destroy us or enrich us. One hesitates to say anything about this characteristic of power as we stand on the threshold of the uses of atomic power. I have to keep reminding myself that atomic power has always been here and that all we have done (and that's a-plenty, I assure you) has been to discover it. I have to remind myself also that we are only on the threshold. What are the powers still untapped of which these first discoveries may be just the slightest hints? And I need to be reminded that we shall not really control these powers at all; our real problem will be to control ourselves. Recognizing these powers for what they are and what they can do, we must learn obedience. I suspect that only that other indefinable, invisible, inviolable Power can possibly help us here— the Power of the Holy Spirit—and we have hardly even tried that Power.

Closely akin to inviolability is a fourth characteristic; power is *invincible*. What really is that drop in temperature that turns water into the ice which can split a wall of granite? How shall we think of this power or these powers? Once in Egypt I was taken to the great rock quarries from which the stone had been cut for the temples of Karnak and Luxor. It was explained to us there that the ancients had understood how to drive wooden wedges into openings made in the rock; these wedges were then soaked with water; as the wedges expanded the rock was split. What was this power? Could the ancients have defined this power? Nevertheless they *used* this power because they knew that it would *always* work. Their ancestors had witnessed to this amazing power and had passed on the word, explained its use, and this witness and use were passed on from one generation to another. For another slant on this we watch the same kind of power let loose in the spring of the year. A little root can split a rock or destroy the usefulness of a drainage pipe. We think we know what we are talking about when we use words like "osmosis" and "capillary attraction," but who shall say that he understands what is taking place in the processes that these words name for us? What powers or kinds of powers are here represented? We do not understand these processes just because we can name them; yet they show themselves invincible as the seasons come and go.

One final trait of power is this: it becomes known

when it is *invested*. It is only when it is invested that it does become useful. What we are accustomed to call human progress has been in a large measure governed, not by the invention of power itself, but by the discovery of powers and the laws of powers and by obedience to the laws of powers in their use. It is significant here, I think, that in the first chapter of Acts, when those early disciples were trying to solve some riddles about their future—will the kingdom be restored at this time—they were not given to know "the times and the seasons." Neither, I suppose are we. But, said Jesus, "Ye shall receive power . . . and ye shall be my witness." That was to be their program for the future: not a series of answers, but a gift of the power of the Holy Spirit *as they witnessed*. It was not power in general, not power as an object of study or something a man could muse about in a theological library, but the gift of power in the obedience of witnessing. The power had to be invested as it was being given. Said Oliver Cromwell in another context, "I never received guidance until I needed it."

An archaeologist of a former day, Melvin G. Kyle, was addressing some of us at a meeting years ago at Muskingum College. He spoke these wisely humorous words: "We all pray for the Holy Spirit, but as soon as the tongues of flame begin to appear we all run for the fire department." So it is with so many of us so much of the time. We think of the Holy Spirit as an interesting study, like stamp collecting or old guns—religion we say with great condescension, can be a very "interesting subject." The Holy Spirit will have none of this compromising attitude. We are in the very plainest sense "playing with fire" here. One ought not to "monkey around" with electricity or with atomic power; how much less with the power of Almighty God. When the early church prayed for long earnest days for the coming of the Holy Spirit they did so according to the command and promise of Christ, not according to neat definitions and careful word studies. And when the Holy Spirit came upon them in power it was in surprising ways no one could control: wind and fire and the shaking of houses to their foundations. They hadn't counted on that sort of thing. But what a witness there was that day!

All we have said so far is by way of showing how possible, indeed how necessary, is a view of truth in which we recognize that neat weights and measurements in the laboratory and the constant testing by our five senses can be quite secondary in the grasp of some kinds of fundamental realities. Whole areas of truth are beyond our description or analysis except as these truths bear witness to themselves through other media. We remind ourselves again that certain tools which are very useful in solving one kind of problem will not solve another problem. You can take a tire iron which is useful for fixing a tire and even useful for beating a man over the head; but it is hardly an instrument for getting at a man's id or super ego. Whole areas of truth are beyond ordinary tools of learning and understanding, beyond easy ways of description and analysis. They must always bear witness to themselves through other media. So it is in the understanding of the Holy Spirit. He is *indefinable, invisible, inviolable, invincible,* and always *invested*—not as we please, but as He pleases.

It has been an assumption of mine for a good many years, and a surprising discovery for some of my classes that as we set ourselves to examine God we suddenly become aware that he is examining us. When we try to make what we like to think is a completely objective and unbiased study of Jesus Christ we have to look steadily into his eyes, only to discover that he is looking steadily into ours. Who then becomes subject and who object? So examine Christ as you will: you will discover him examining you. Flesh and blood did not reveal Christ to you any more than flesh and blood revealed him to Peter at the time of the Great Confession. The Holy Spirit then and now takes of the things of Christ and shows them unto us. Spiritual things are spiritually discerned and with that discernment will come the kind of self-knowledge to make a man cry out, "Depart from me for I am a sinful man." In revealing Christ to us the Holy Spirit will search our hearts. Then we shall see who is being studied and analyzed.

These things are profoundly true of our study of the Spirit of God. We may examine the evidence for his existence, tabulate the ways in which he is described in Scripture, argue for his personality, place him neatly in the Trinity. All these exercises take their proper place in our studies. In such study we need all the intellectual acumen of which we are capable. It is of the essence of Protestantism that these things should be studied and defined as far as our minds and understandings can take us. But finally, and perhaps sooner than we expect, and in ways we haven't suspected, the Holy Spirit will be dealing with us more than we are dealing with him. He is the initiator and sustainer of truth, even truth about himself. Understand him as we may, it behooves us rather to hear him, obey him, and know him best when his life surges through our own, empowering us to know other truth, and sending us out to be witnesses in Jerusalem and Judea and in Samaria even, and to the uttermost parts of the earth.

Jesus had a wonderful word of promise about the Spirit. "If ye then being evil know how to give good gifts to your children, how much more shall your Heavenly Father give the Holy Spirit to them that ask him." We can ask for the Holy Spirit and he is promised to us. The only real question in all this is: Do we really want him?

Chapter Ten

THE WORK OF THE HOLY SPIRIT

IN THE LAST CHAPTER WE RECOGNIZED THE DIFFICULTY
of understanding the nature of the Holy Spirit and
tried to explain this difficulty in several ways: we ourselves are not purely spiritual beings and therefore the
Holy Spirit is a person not exactly like us and hence difficult to explain in our ordinary experiences. Even
when we do approach the Holy Spirit for study we discover that he keeps pointing our attention to the truth
of Christ rather than to the truth concerning himself.
Since one of his offices is to bring us to repentance it is
frequently our experience that where we would try to
pass a judgment on the Holy Spirit by examining him
we become aware that the process has been reversed and
he is examining us—in the light of truth, the light is on
us! In order to help us understand such phenomena we
shifted ground into areas in which we have some

familiarity and where we believe we have some grasp of the realities and thought for a little on the phenomenon of power, particularly the power of electricity. From this analogy we concluded that such characteristics as bother us in understanding the Holy Spirit are characteristics which we find quite acceptable in our grasp of other powers, characteristics such as lack of clear definition, invisibility, invincibility and the like. Accepting what the Bible tells us of the Holy Spirit as spirit and power we then found it easier to understand how these things which the Bible reveals can be so.

In this chapter in which we discuss the *work* of the Holy Spirit we face the same kind of problem: how does a thing like a spirit work? Have we any experiences which we take for granted which will help us to understand other experiences which on the face of it seem quite beyond our understanding? In a world which seems quite evidently material is there a place for spiritual realities?

A good starting place is an examination of that world which seems so material, so completely physical. Physicists are telling us that the material world can be divided and sub-divided into much smaller bits of stuff than we normally would believe. When I was in college we took molecules for granted; they were the bits of stuff which served as the building blocks of the material world. We were then led to consider the makeup of the molecule and were taught that the molecules are made up of electrons whizzing their ways around the protons at the center of their systems. The end is not yet because the protons themselves seem capable of further sub-divisions. But the structure of the electron whirling around the proton will serve our purposes for illustration. All things are made of this elemental stuff but there is a way in which this elemental stuff is not "stuff" in the usual sense of the word at all. What we find is not a static thing at all but a dynamic relationship. The whole universe is actually in a whirl, and the various elements are capable of almost infinite combinations and re-combinations into all the things which are apparent to us in the ordinary everyday uses of our senses. The chief characteristic of this stuff does not seem to be stuff or matter at all but energy, and what we see and handle in the physical world is really this dynamic sort of thing combined in certain ways to make what now appears. It could all be rearranged into entirely different things. What is needed is the feeding into this dynamic structure some creativity, some act of will, some dominating idea which will make different things out of the basic things, the basic elements with which we have to work. Thus two things are evident: matter is more like energy than material (at least material as we usually think of it); this matter becomes what it is or can be changed into something else by another energy which is not material at all—the power of an idea, for example. If, as some scientists have suggested, even the various elements can be reduced finally to the hydrogen element, with the simple structure of just one electron circling one proton, we can see how relatively important and fundamental is the idea or thought by which this one atom can be built up, made more complex, combined and re-combined, into all the wonders of what is evident to the naked eye, wonders which seem so fixed and so settled. In fact we count on our whole universe as a thing, or a combination of things, whereas, in the deepest sense, it is really the expression of some rich, complex, creative idea.

As I write this I am working at a desk. The desk could have a wide variety of structures and still be a desk. It could be rearranged and re-combined, have things added or subtracted, and still serve as a desk. This illustrates the changes possible in a basic idea by the play of more complex ideas. But go deeper. The *material* of the desk can be subjected to all kinds of ideas. I can break it up into kindling; that would be simple. Now I can burn the wood and end up with at least ashes and heat in addition to other by-products. The heat can be applied to something else; it can be changed into the power of a steam engine, it can cook my hamburgers, it can put people to sleep in a stuffy room. Let your imagination run as it will and ask yourself what further changes can be produced by the products of this heat—the engine, the hamburgers, the stuffy room—and so on out as far as your mind can go. Or look at the ashes and see what can be done with them. Ashes are good for tomato plants; people eat tomatoes; what people eat can be changed in subtle and miraculous fashion into ideas in peoples' heads which can be either wise or foolish, creative or destructive. Let your mind run awhile in that direction. What started as a relatively simple structure, a desk, has now the infinite possibilities of not only almost endless other products (material things) but even endless kinds of thoughts (spiritual things), which in turn can think about what to do with other desks.

Several facts are now apparent. At the heart of the universe we find energy as basic, and perhaps more basic than stuff. The shaping of the universe in all its variety is definitely related to the energizing of a spiritual rather than of a material nature, and this thought or spirit which energizes is the crucial reality as over against the secondary reality of the material on which it works. Ideas create things. But more important even than that: ideas create other ideas; men and movements are based on motives. Motives can be shared, motives can be introduced where there was no motive; motives may come into conflict.

I have always been amazed at the miracle of speech, a gift most of us have and a gift most of us don't think much about. Take time to trace out the miracle of speech from this approach which we have just been emphasizing—the interrelation between spirit or idea and the physical body—the basic importance of the idea as against the material. An idea arises in my mind (that is almost miracle enough!) and I tell it to you. That's simple enough; at least, it is habitual enough. But watch it. Idea which is non-physical is able to flutter the vocal chords in my throat with the most amazing and complex combinations of pitch, timbre, inflection and control to give a wide variety of symbols which have common acceptance as speech in the particular acceptance of a given language. What was non-physical in my brain has become physical in my throat. Vibrations go out into the air and fall on your ears. The vibrations may fall on many ears and different people may react in a wide variety of ways to what I am saying. But to keep the illustration as simple as possible—the vibrations fall on your ears, vibrations of a special kind are set up inside your ears, nerves of a specialized function are "stimulated" by the vibrations and the nerve "stimuli" eventually convey, still physically, this message of mine until in a most wonderful and hidden way, these "stimuli" become an idea in your brain. My idea is now your idea; what was not in your thinking before is now in your thinking. If we can imagine a simple idea like "Let's walk a little faster," the simple idea now expresses itself in your physical body in physical ways and all kinds of different things take place in your body as *you* quicken your step. But suppose I am a top sergeant shouting out marching orders; suppose my orders are a call to attack. Now the results begin to move toward infinite possibilities again.

Adolf Hitler with his terrible raucous voice began

shouting ideas to masses of German people. Soon millions were on the march on the offense, soon millions were on the march on defense, ships and trucks and trains were on the move, ideas were translated into books, newspaper headlines took on a different hue and cry, nations and kingdoms were moved, history was changed, and the end is not yet. The significance of Hitler may help us to see the significance of something else. A Galilean, virtually unknown beyond his own immediate circle, an itinerant rabbi walking and talking in a beaten-up back country of the Roman Empire, caused such an upheaval that the whole world eventually set its calendars by his birth. What did he do? Well, ask Peter. "To whom shall we go? Thou hast the *words* of eternal life." In the Fourth Gospel we have some interesting philosophizing on all this. "In the beginning was the Word"—logos, idea, clue, scheme, pattern—what God had to say to men. "The Word became flesh and dwelt among us"—Christ the Living Word speaking the wonderful words of life—and as the epistle reflects, "That which we have seen and handled of the word of life declare we unto you that you might have fellowship with us." Here was the miracle of the Great Idea, what God had been saying in so many times and places "in these last days" He has spoken to us in His Son. The thought took form in the physical world, the thought took form in audible speech, and now all this is declared to us that we might have our place in the fellowship. It is the miracle of speech on the grand

[135]

scale—and the end is not yet. There is something in store "beyond anything we could ask or think," "eye hath not seen. . . ."

Our simple illustrations have led us to some rather deeper thinking on things that frequently seem so ordinary. One more illustration is needed. You have seen many times what I now relate. The members of a certain football team once came into the dressing room at half time utterly defeated. The score wasn't too bad yet, but neither the players individually nor the team as a unit had what it took to turn the game in the other direction. Things were running downhill. The coach gave them a "pep talk" between halves and they went out a *new* team and won the game. It's an old, old story but needs to be told again. How did they become a *new* team? It's hard to say just by recording what happened. They didn't change their uniforms; they didn't eat a hearty meal; they didn't try some more exercises to get in shape; there was no change in the number and total tonnage of the team. What happened and just how were they a new team? Simple enough—if you can do it! The coach had in him what he put into the team, or he tapped what was in the school (school *spirit*—is that a reality?) and conveyed that to them. How? By a series of words. But that series of words that had been in him was now in them. To say that this was not the greatest reality in the second half of the game is to forget that the remainder of the afternoon was bruising physical combat as the first half had been, but with a different spirit. The spirit which had not been in them was now in them. Nothing else made the difference. Let's not be nebulous, you say, let's talk about the realities; it's what's in the score book that counts. How true. Now then, what did make the difference in the score? What makes the difference in any score, assuming we even know what game we are playing!

Please make no more of these analogies than they are worth. What I am trying to say in a variety of ways is merely this: the whole area of the non-physical as against the material has its own reality; this reality is more basic and important than the material on which it works; spiritual realities can be introduced and used in many more ways than we have ever dreamed of; the universe as we look upon it so superficially is "wide open" to the ministries of the spiritual. We ought to be ready now to accept what the Bible tells us: that the Holy Spirit of God can and does find entrance into this physical world. It is the sort of thing we ought to expect, knowing what we happen to know at this stage of our discoveries about the structure of this amazing planet which we inhabit.

The Holy Spirit of God works when and where and how he pleases. He enlivens and quickens the whole physical universe, and we have seen it is possible for the things of the spirit so to do. He lies at the basis of what we like to call "bright ideas" which arise in our minds in such strange ways. He is therefore able to inspire certain men in special ways. He can touch our minds with thought about things in ways which the things themselves might not; thus he takes of the things of Christ and shows them unto us. He is the Spirit of Truth who guides us into truth; all truth is God's truth coming as it does from God the Spirit of Truth. And because he is a Person he can penetrate our spirits in personal ways leading to personal understandings and reactions. Why should this thought be incredible to any of us? It is the sort of thing great friends and great lovers experience all the time. Walking together because "they agree," they know, they simply *know*, what the other person is thinking without the necessity of speech or gesture, in their singleness of spirit. Why is it thought incredible that the Spirit of God can penetrate our thoughts directly when we are not aghast at the miraculous way in which we penetrate one another's thoughts by so many indirections? Which is the greater miracle? Does not the normal way by which we "reach" each other make the other way seem even more possible?

Endless are the ministries of the Spirit as he touches our lives. Look for a moment at a few of them. The Spirit converts, he ministers, he guides, he comforts.

The Holy Spirit converts. In a multitude of ways which we do not know (the secret operation of the Holy Spirit in regeneration, in the implanting of a new life principle) we come to the consciousness that life must be turned about. We have been traveling in one direction and now we must travel in another direction;

we looked at life in one way, now we must look at it in another way; literally we turn around—we are converted. Usually this conversion experience is thought of in two ways: repentance and faith. Repentance is usually thought of as more negative—we give up certain things; faith as more positive—we lay hold on certain things. I think the two words, or rather the experiences they define, overlap and inter-relate. Repentance is not a negative word at all in its basic sense. It means (repensir, pepenser) to "rethink." A repentance takes place when we have to *think* of the totality of life in a brand new way. In such a sense we are new creatures, we have had a new birth. We rethink life in this new way because we have come upon a new fact. If, for example, it should suddenly turn out to be true that the moon actually is made of green cheese, then we would all have to repent. We would have to rethink something that up to this time we considered utter foolishness and begin to think about it as sober truth. A great many other ideas and values would now have to come under some careful re-examination. A new fact has made us rethink (re-pent) many many things.

The fact of Christ leads us to that kind of repentance and the Holy Spirit shows us the fact of Christ. Now we must repent. Suddenly we see what God is like; now we see what man should be; now we have a clear and honest judgment on sin which can no longer be thought of as an evolutionary over-hang or something just too too sophisticated; now we re-assess our values and our goals;

[139]

and because values and goals have changed we change all our ways of life. The Kingdom of God puts the kingdoms of this world in proper perspective. Now what about our ambitions? Now what really counts in life? This is our repentance. How much deeper this is than just "being sorry" for something we have done. Being sorry now means that we know "godly sorrow," sorrow with the love of God as our point of reference. We have sinned against God, not against ourselves or against society. A man doesn't have to believe in Jesus Christ, but if he does believe in him he *has* to repent; "old things are passed away, all things have become new."

We see now the basic positive quality in repentance, the positive note in our conversion, the inter-relatedness of repentance with faith. It is because we have faith in Christ and because faith works that we are led to repentance. We are baptized with water indicative of the old things which need to be washed away, but we are baptized with the Spirit which now moves us to new things. It is no use getting rid of one devil if seven more come in. The space left empty by the removal of that devil must be filled up with the activity of the Spirit of God. So many Christians assess their Christianity in terms of things they don't do. But a dead man does nothing at all. Is that Christianity? To even suggest it is nonsense. What then is Christianity? It is to be in a saving relationship to God through Jesus Christ, and when the way is made open through Him, we are converted by the ministry of the Spirit. Thus we repent, assessing the whole of life in terms of this Christ on whom we lay hold in faith.[5] Can you imagine what would happen to all of life if only Christian lives were marked by the rethinking of everything—home, business, society, leisure—in the light of the fact of Christ, in whom we say we have faith! The Holy Spirit converts us—turns us around—by showing us Christ, in whom we now have faith and because of whom we now repent.

The Holy Spirit ministers. He speaks of the things of Christ according to our condition. He ministers to our needs, but always to our deepest needs. We think we need many things; if we had Christ in our hearts would we have so many other needs? The Holy Spirit ministers Christ to us. How rich such an idea may be, how rich the reality of the experience itself! Much of modern life is marked by emptiness and purposelessness. One of our modern poets speaks of "the God-shaped vacuum" in man; a very recent book by Emile Cailliet faces the question of how to put purpose back into life. Read modern novels and plays to comprehend the sickness of the empty heart. We try to "get at" ourselves in a variety of ways and the psychiatrist helps us with his methods. We are trying to get at the wellsprings of life to see if things can be refreshed there; what bubbles up seems to speak of poisoned springs. But the Holy Spirit of God can touch us where we cannot touch ourselves, to fill us with life where we have become lifeless. He can heal us where we most need

---

[5] We expanded on the idea of faith in the last chapter.

healing. How desperately we work on ourselves and on each other—buck up, play the man, get hold of yourself, think of something else, think positively, quit worrying, forget it. Great salves these are! Can't we see that we are addressing ourselves to the very center of life when there is no center, or where the center is the disease? How can we say buck up when the "Bucker-Upper" himself needs to be bucked up? How can we say "play the man," when the player himself is prostrate? Who shall minister to us there? There is a simple prayer for a simple therapy: "Lord fill me with Thyself, heal the place where I can't touch, create in me a clean heart." Surely we know that "the issues of life" come from the heart. The Holy Spirit cleanses our hearts.

The Holy Spirit guides. I wonder whether anyone can really make up his mind on anything if he makes sure first of all to take every factor into consideration. Oh, I know we have to make decisions and that we can't live a day without decisions. But just how wise are all those decisions? You would think, wouldn't you, that no decision would be really wise unless every possible angle could be judged first. Does anyone know every possible angle? Is all the evidence ever in? Is it given to man to know the complete inter-relatedness of everything with everything else? To ask the questions is to answer them. No one is wise enough for all these things. What then shall be our clue? How can we walk with confidence? Must we spend all our days with our hand to the plow but still looking back? How perfectly evident it is then, whether we accept it or not, that we do walk by some kind of faith. But faith in what? Well, more than we know, faith in the fact that underneath are the everlasting arms; somehow the loose ends which we must leave strewn around are caught up, the dropped stitch is worked again into the design. But how much better first to commit one's way to Him. How much better to seek His guidance and rest in His promises. The Holy Spirit leads us to seek his guiding, he leads us into truth as we reach for decision, he honors our choices as they are committed to God.

The Holy Spirit comforts. He is called the Paraclete, the one who stands by our side. We should expect his companionship in our hours of distress. Since he is the Comforter Christ promised to his disciples when it was necessary for him to go away, we can reasonably expect that his comforting will be Christ-like. This would be all of a man's desiring. The word comfort, however, is not a soft word, no matter how much it may have taken on that meaning. It has the same meaning as fortification; we are to be "comfortified" i.e., "strengthened around." When we have done all, the Holy Spirit still keeps us standing. The Holy Spirit our Comforter is our Strength, the strength to take suffering and abuse, the strength to stand up to life, the strength to stand for the right. Or try this: he is comforting strength; he is strengthening comfort: and that's what we have been wanting all the time.

So much for the works of the Spirit, and briefly for all

that. What about our works? How do we know we have
the Spirit? First, because, increasingly we come to know
Christ; second, because increasingly we live in and desire to live in the truth, for He is the Spirit of Truth;
finally, and here we can test ourselves rather sharply,
because we have the fruits of the Spirit. They are surprising fruit—"love, joy, peace, patience, kindness, goodness, faithfulness, gentleness, self-control." Not much
room here for all our anxieties and cantankerousness.
Most of us by such standards are still this side of life
in the Spirit.

Chapter Eleven

THE CHURCH

WHEN YOU LOOK AT THE CHURCH WHAT DO YOU SEE?
What do you see first? The Church is made up of people, buildings, organizations, institutions, philanthro-
pies, councils and committees—and committees! Our
problem is to understand the Church, if possible, in its
simplicity, to see what is essential and to see what is
added on. It was suggested that the Roman Church was
a great ship which had been collecting barnacles for
centuries and that the Reformation was an attempt to
scrape off the barnacles to get at the original structure.
The fact is we can understand the Church best, that is,
in its simplicity, when we do see it at the Reformation
era. With the exception of the day on which the Church
started out from Pentecost there is no other time in
history when the Church, as such, was being examined
so seriously to see what, essentially, a church *is*.

The Reformers, especially Luther and Calvin, had
forced upon them the necessity of analyzing the Church

and establishing the Church afresh as against the Roman Church of their day. At the same time they had to fight against the schismatics who, seeing that Protestantism had revolted against Rome, believed that they too had the right to revolt against their own church. In establishing their position between Romanism and sectarianism the Reformers had to construct a doctrine of the Church that could stand up to attack from either side.

Luther's doctrine of the Church began with the simplicity and reality of his own deep personal religious experience. Luther had been born into and nurtured by the Roman Church. As an Augustinian monk in that church, he had sought by all the disciplines of his order to find the assurance of his salvation for which he so earnestly longed. He did not find such assurance, and the history of his monkish asceticisms is a piteous commentary on the poverty of any salvation by works. In constant obedience and in constant soul searchings, he found no peace. Even his great-hearted father-confessor, Staupitz, could not lead him to the joy of salvation.

Thus the matter stood when, in the providence of God, Luther was called upon to give lectures based on the books of Psalms, Romans and Galatians. With this teaching came the necessity and opportunity for deep study in these books, and with this study came the "illumination," his discovery that his salvation was not a question of his works but a justification by God, a declaration of his new standing before God, based not on his own righteousness but on "the righteousness of God," received "by faith alone." The keystone of his theology became "justification by faith." In Psalm 22 where is found imbedded the cry of Christ, "Why hast thou forsaken me?" Luther discovered that all his sins and all his guilt had been borne by Christ the Saviour. In Galatians he came to understand the poverty of works and the truth of salvation by grace alone. In Romans he learned of "the righteousness of God," the free gift of God made possible through the perfect obedience and substitutionary atonement of Christ. With such knowledge came assurance and peace. In his new-found union with Christ was a saving relationship which no man had given to him and which certainly no man could take away.

We must see plainly what happened to Luther. He now experienced salvation apart from the hierarchy and the ecclesiastical machinery of the visible church. The Church of Rome had not given him this assurance of his standing with God and could not now control it or destroy it. He began to understand, therefore, that whatever is meant by the Church as the body of Christ of which Christ is the head, it cannot be limited or defined by that series of churchly stratifications which finds its peak finally in the pope. What then is the Church?

To Luther two things were now clear: first, salvation is a direct relationship with God through Jesus Christ; second, the means by which this relationship is established is the Scriptures. He began to suspect something else; whereas he now possessed this wonderful personal experience himself, and whereas he rejoiced in the Scriptures by which this experience had been mediated to him, there was still another matter: a man cannot be a church by himself in a kind of individual mystical vacuum. The Church is not one person; it is a body with many members. There must be, Luther reasoned, others who experience this same relationship, mediated by the same Scriptures, this union with Christ. If he has union with Christ and if others have union with Christ, then this union is somehow the essence of the Church as the body of Christ. If, then, he and others are united "in Christ" they must in some wonderful way be "in" one another. Union with Christ is creative of communion; joined together with Christ they *must* be joined together with one another. This communion with Christ and thus with one another is the Church.

It is believed that the term "invisible church" began with Bucer, but the fact of the invisible church was already a part of Luther's experience and understanding. This Church as he originally conceived it is the whole company of believers known only to God wherever they may be found in history or wherever they may now be scattered across the face of the earth. This idea of the "invisible" church is still a constant in our discussions of the nature of the church today. There is this numerous company, known finally to God alone,

[148]

in congregations, denominations, churches; these constitute the actual Church of Christ.

However "invisible" this company of believers may
be, we must constantly remind ourselves that the
Church is still made up of men and women of flesh
and blood and that it cannot therefore really remain
invisible, because men and women live in the flesh;
and as members of the Church of Christ it is in the
flesh that they will carry out their functions as church
members. This hidden body of true believers must in
some fashion find expression in mission and in life;
and as soon as they thus express themselves they must
show themselves in visible ways. There is, therefore,
and by necessity, a "visible" Church of which the members known only to God are among the members, and
in which the true members of Christ find ways and
means of fulfilling their Christian life and witness.
The "invisible" Church must by its very nature and
because of the nature of mankind show itself finally as
the "visible" Church.

Watch now as the Church begins to act out its inner
life in the external world. Luther had had his own
religious experience through the ministry of the Word.
But the ministry of the Word had not stopped with
the original transformation or conversion of Luther.
After his "illumination" he had been nurtured by this
same Word. Therefore, there was laid upon the
Church as an endless responsibility the necessity of
the teaching and preaching of the Word. The Refor-

mation Church began to discover what we take for granted now, that the total work of the total Church is somehow related to the ministry of this Word of God. Vieth of Yale, writing on Christian education, has this most suggestive description of the Church's task: "to confront with and control by the Gospel of Jesus Christ." Thus we see the double responsibility and the double difficulty of the program of the Church. There are many for whom the first step is necessary: they must be confronted with the Gospel in order to make a decision. Then there are the others who need to be nurtured in the very faith into which they have been born. When we remember that every person is at a different stage in his Christian pilgrimage, then the task of the proper ministry of the Word becomes very complex indeed. Thus there is the necessity for all kinds of programs—the total work of the total Church—in order to confront and control by the Gospel. Such responsibilities are not only congregational but denominational; soon institutions must be created for specialized purposes related to fundamental tasks of the Church. As complexity increases we still look, as Luther and Calvin did, for the two marks of the Church, two "notae": the Word is preached, and the sacraments are administered. However complex the Church may become in the necessities of its organizations, if the Word is preached and the sacraments administered, we may know for sure that the Church —the real Church, the Church finally known only to

God—is there, never lost in its visible complexities.

The Church is also under the responsibilities of the Great Commission and it must therefore take on the visible machinery and complex organization which world mission requires. The Church is not simply a place *to* which people come for the hearing of the Word, for common worship and praise. It is a place *from* which people go out commissioned for a task. However simple the original faith may be by which these people are brought into their saving relationship with God through Christ, this yearning for the simple gospel can give them no escape from the complex pressures of this world in which we live; to go out with a mission to that world at all necessitates many burdens, many ambiguities; the simplicities become somewhat confusing. But our safeguard in all our "churchmanship" is this: however necessary all the machinery is (and I underline that necessity again and again), it is still only machinery. It is not therefore to be confused with the Christian experience itself, the Christian experience which makes its existence necessary in the first place, and for which alone it is to be used. There are people who are frightened by organization, who withdraw from its necessity and therefore neglect its use; there are others who appear to think the organization is an end in itself and who get a little nervous over too much "spirituality." But the Church is first and fundamentally a spiritual reality, the reality of our communion with God and so with one another, and this reality *by its own inner necessity* brings the organized visible church into existence. The two are interlocked but not to be confused. Our problem, is this: to keep inspiriting the organization.

It comes as a surprise to many to discover that Luther and Calvin both believed that the Church must express itself in society; requirements of the Church are not limited to the preaching of the Gospel. As nearly as we can discover, this idea of the Church as a means of conditioning the social and political relationships of Christians was never even debatable. It was assumed that the Church ought to be a creative power in all society—in home relationships, in business ethics, in political responsibilities. In short, as Luther construed the Church, the invisible Church must become visible not only in the congregations and the denominations of the people of God but in the creation of a Christian culture, a "Volk," a people of God, living in and developing community life, community standards, Christian law and order.

Let us review for a moment now how this idea of the Church has grown. It started with actual Christian experience between the believer and his Lord. People with this common religious experience found themselves together in one spirit, united for worship and the ministry of the Word. In such an organization, simple as it might be, there was the commission to bring others into this saving relationship and to teach men how to be Christian in all their human relationships. We were led to see how this spiritual fellowship must by its nature take on a visible and organized structure. The church group meets at a certain place at a certain time. That means a meetinghouse of some kind. The meetinghouse means some kind of financing; heating, plumbing, janitor service—such things begin to become requirements of the Church. Preaching means preachers and that means colleges and seminaries; sacraments mean administrators of the sacraments and that means ordination and those who ordain; preparation for church membership means teachers; care of the poor means deacons; government means elders. Yes, it is fundamental that the true Church is made up of believers known finally to God alone; yet this company of believers known only to God must, in the nature of the case, organize in visible groups to do physical, mechanical, social things.

It is suspected by all of us, I am sure, that not all church members are true believers. Every worshiper in a given place on a given Sunday morning is not, we suspect, a true believer. Some are half devoted, some are not yet ready for full Christian experience, some are hidden or manifest or subtle or gross sinners. But who is able to separate the sheep from the goats? The Reformers tried by various schemes of discipline to purify the visible Church in terms of the ideal invisible Church. Excommunication was the method by which they attempted to keep the Church pure, in spite of the fact that they knew perfectly well that the visible

Church would never be completely pure. Luther was more easily satisfied on this score than was Calvin. He believed in the creative and nuturing power of the Word. He believed that if the Word is properly preached and if the sacraments are properly administered, one can be assured that true Christians are present and that in due time, under the ministry of the Word, the purity of the Church will take care of itself.

Calvin began with the same foundations as did Luther but he moved to more stringent organization. He too believed in the whole company of the elect known only to God, and this is the emphasis he gives to the Church in his first edition of the *Institutes* in 1536. His experiences in Geneva, then in Strasbourg, then in Geneva again, to which we cannot turn aside in this type of treatment, tested his theory of the "invisible" Church against the demands of the community, the strength of the Church as an organization as over against other nonchurch organizations—the State, for example. He felt that he had to know who and what the Church is. Thus, increasingly, his various editions of the *Institutes* reflect his feeling after sharp definition for the visible organized Church. He never lost sight of the fundamental "hiddenness" of the true Church, but he was in a situation where the visible Church in the beleaguered city of Geneva was fighting for its very existence and he simply had to know who would stand up to be counted. We have to understand the problem at least: looseness in relationship to the Church in the city of Geneva was not only possible heresy but definite betrayal. In a situation where you either hang together or hang separately you have to be able to count *members!* By the time Calvin had moved from his first edition of the *Institutes* of 1536 to his last and definitive edition of 1559, his discussion of the "visible" Church had moved from incidental comment to one hundred pages of close argument. Almost Harnack persuadeth us, "Theory follows practice in church government!"

Sharing as he did Luther's great religious experience and zeal, Calvin was nevertheless an ecclesiastical statesman. He knew that the Church must show itself in structure and order to accomplish mission. The late B. L. Manning of Oxford has expressed this well:

Calvin perceived that the greatest need of the sixteenth century was a positive ecclesiastical policy. It was idle to criticize the old Church in the manner of Wyclif. It was insufficient to arouse fresh piety among men in the manner of Luther. Only a Church with a claim and sphere as wide, an authority as august, a foundation as venerable and secure, a machinery as efficient, a policy as subtle, a temper as high, a mission as complete, could replace the corrupted Church of Rome and hold its own against the secular state rising everywhere on the ruins of mediaeval religion. Protestantism . . . had not yet produced an ecclesiastical statesman, an architect on earth of that city whose builder and maker is God. In Calvin it produced him.[6]

Thus Calvin understood and established the structure of the Church visible. But he never lost sight of the "whole company of believers known only to God." He never lost sight of the fact that the reality of the Church depends on the reality of the experience of salvation; the Church begins with a confession of faith and never loses that confession. Our danger today is that we accept the church organization which has been passed on to us in our Protestant heritage and get men and women to "join Church" without any understanding of the primary religious *experience* (not information) which lies at the basis of our communion with God and with one another. This religious experience must be brought into existence by the ministry of the Word and Spirit. It is this religious experience which we must look for in its creation and nurture, and no organization, however beautiful it may look on a wall chart, can take the place of religious experience. The whole complex of ecclesiastical machinery, however essential in a secondary way, has only one primary assignment: to make available the means by which religious experience can be initiated and strengthened.

[6] This quotation was given to me by Dr. John S. Whale, my supervisor at Cambridge University. Since then Dr. Whale has used the substance of this quotation in his book *The Protestant Tradition*, Cambridge University Press, 1955, pp. 125-126. There he gives credit in a footnote to B. L. Manning, *The Making of Modern English Religion*, Student Christian Movement Press, London, 1929, pp. 95.

The "invisible" Church is the true body of Christ of which he is the Head; the "visible" Church gives the hands and the feet.

Conversely, in our concern for the purity of the Church in terms of religious experience and total commitment, the Reformers remind us that it is also of the essence of the Church that the invisible must take on visible forms in many places and in many ways. We must accept, and continue to purify, the visible church with all its rich variety albeit sometimes back-breaking machinery.

Chapter Twelve

THE SACRAMENTS

AT ONE TIME OR ANOTHER IN THE HISTORY OF THE church seven rites have been looked upon as sacraments. These seven rites are Baptism, the Lord's Supper, Confirmation, Penance, Holy Orders, Marriage, and Extreme Unction. Of these seven practices Protestants now hold that only two are Sacraments: Baptism and the Lord's Supper. The Roman church recognizes all seven and at one time the Reformer Luther recognized three.[7] The fact that Protestants now hold to only two sacraments can mean only one thing: namely, the Protestants have settled on certain requirements for a sacrament which exclude all other acts except Baptism and the Lord's Supper from classification as sacraments. It is instructive, therefore, to see what requirements the Protestants demand as essential to a sacrament; instructive in telling us why they choose

---

[7] Unpublished manuscript, James Harper, late professor of Xenia Seminary, c.f. H. T. Kerr, Jr., A Compend of Luther's Theology.

only two sacraments, instructive in telling us what a sacrament is.

1. *A sacrament must be of direct divine appointment.* We believe that worship in all its parts must be regulated by the commands of God. Since the Lord through the Scripture is our sole lawgiver, no man or body of men has the right to devise any religious exercise, especially one designed to symbolize or convey divine realities. God alone can introduce ordinances to which he can give his blessing. It is quite clear that Baptism and the Lord's Supper were instituted by Christ, the one on the occasion of the Great Commission just before the Ascension and the other on the night before his crucifixion. The necessity for such a divine appointment is plainly suggested in the words with which the Apostle Paul introduces his account of the Lord's Supper in I Corinthians 11:23: "For *I have received of the Lord* that which also *I delivered* unto you. . . ." It is at the point of divine Scriptural appointment that we so often part company with the Romanists and never more clearly than here where we decide what is and what is not properly a sacrament; they are satisfied to take as authoritative the findings of the Roman Church during its long, tortuous, and often confused history. On the contrary, we search, and in vain, for Biblical authority for such practices as Extreme Unction or Penance.

2. *In valid sacraments there are certain sensible signs, sensible to sight and touch.* Words alone do not

constitute a sacrament although they stand closely related to it. More than audible verbal signs are required in a sacrament; other senses are also used. At the same time this word of warning must be introduced: sacraments can become over-mysterious to the point of magic or "dumb show" unless frequently and even normally, the spoken word, not only of institution but also of explanation, accompanies the sensible signs.

3. *The sensible signs must also be by appointment of God if they are to convey proper content.* The content of the sacraments has to do with spiritual blessings and duties, and the signs must symbolize such blessings and duties. The signs are linked with our salvation. In no other way can we fully understand such language as this: "Repent and be baptized"; or "For as many of you as have been baptized into Christ have put on Christ"; or "this is my body broken for you . . . this do in remembrance of me."

4. *A sacrament is a sealing ordinance to all who rightly receive it.* It forms a pledge to those who receive the sacrament of the actual gift of the blessings which it signifies. Circumcision in the Old Testament, which is parallel to Baptism in the New Testament, is actually called "a seal of the righteousness of faith. . . ." This is not to say that the sign is the blessing or even to insist that the sign carries the blessing in itself, but it is to say that the sign is the assurance that the blessing is now being given. In his way it is a seal, or

[160]

signature, that the God who seals or signs does "make good."

5. *A sacrament is a Church ordinance as distinguished from one of private, family, or even social nature.* It is to be administered only to those who wish to show their separation from the world to God, indicated by a public profession of this new relationship and loyalty. Baptism is a sign of entrance into a new group with new privileges and responsibilities; one is now a member of the family of God through his promises. The Lord's Supper is to nurture and strengthen us in this new life. But always the assumption of our participation in the sacrament is that we are now to be living a new life in a new Body known as the Church, a Body of which Christ is the Head. By definition and by necessity this new Body, the Church, must be different from any other group to which we belong; it is certainly different from the world out of which we have been called. It is careless thinking about this difference between our church citizenship and our world citizenship which makes the Church so worldly.

6. *Participation, and not mere vision, is implied in a sacrament.* A man receives nothing from a sacrament which he merely witnesses being administered to, or received by, others. The elements of the sacrament must be applied according to their nature to the one who is to receive the seal and the benefits which the sign assures.

7. *According to divine appointment there is established a union between the outward sign in the sacrament and the thing signified.* Although the outward sign has been appointed because of its *natural* fitness (water for cleansing, bread for food) to represent the spiritual blessings signified, yet the appointment of God must be added to constitute a true sacramental union between the sign and the thing signified. It is because of this union that there can be an interchange of names between the sign and the things signified. Thus Christ can be called our "Passover"; the bread is called "the body of Christ"; and the cup is termed "the new testament in my blood."

8. *The virtue of a sacrament is not inherent in itself.* Thus the mere participation in a material sense cannot secure the blessing symbolized. Nor does the virtue of the sacrament depend on the inward intention or piety of the one who administers it, but only on the blessing of Christ and the operation of his Spirit in those who rightly receive. Many have been baptized who have never become regenerated, and many have taken part in the Lord's Supper to their condemnation, not discerning the Lord's body.[8]

It will be seen quite clearly that Baptism and the Lord's Supper come under the definition of these

---

[8] This brief outline and briefer comment are based on the unpublished theological lectures of James Harper, late of Xenia Seminary of Xenia, Ohio. The lectures on this and other theological topics are in manuscript form in the Pittsburgh Theological Seminary library.

characteristics of a sacrament. In the other five sacraments of the Roman Church we see the invention of man (even man in church council) and the place of tradition along with Scripture as authority. Apart from the fact that these Roman Catholic practices have no divine authority by appointment by Christ several have another quite evident weakness: they are not available to all Christians. In marriage, for example, a blessing of Christ is available for people who marry which is not available for people who remain single; in holy orders we find priests presumably receiving blessings from Christ which are not available for other non-official Christians. What happens to the "content" of extreme unction when a man meets his death without the benefits of extreme unction? We hold that not only must the sacrament be by divine appointment and in the way it was appointed and with the materials appointed, but that these sacraments are the means of entrance into and nurture in the Christian life available to all who will to be in the Christian life.

Accepting Baptism and the Lord's Supper as rightly constituted sacraments, we can examine certain other characteristics of the sacraments specifically. In Baptism we insist that the covenant promises of God lie at the basis of the sacrament and the sign of Baptism is given to adults as they are able to receive it in repentance and faith. The promises are initiated and sustained by God; repentance and faith are also gifts of God; the sign is to show that the covenant promise has been accepted. When Baptism is administered to infants, the sacrament still rests on the promises of God: promises to believers and to their children. The sign in Baptism signifies that the parents who are believers have believed that the promises are for them and for their children and they receive the promises on behalf of their children. With the reception of the promises go also the vows of the parents that the child will be nurtured in the Christian faith to that day when he shall accept or reject the promises himself. If we keep the idea of the covenant in mind and if we keep in mind that the promises and the acts are initiated and sustained by God, not by men, we need have no great difficulty in moving from adult to infant Baptism and seeing the validity of both.[9]

In the Lord's Supper we recognize again that everything done in the sacrament rests on God's promises and not on men's actions. He has promised his presence and the benefits of the sacrament; there are the visible signs of the bread and the wine according to Christ's practice and command; and there is the spiritual preparation of the recipient by which he is able by faith to receive Christ and his benefits by receiving the bread and the cup. At the place of parental vows in

---

[9] It is completely impossible to debate here the validity of infant baptism. Scores of books have been written. For a good case for infant baptism, see John Murray, *Christian Baptism,* Committee on Christian Education, The Orthodox Presbyterian Church, Philadelphia, Pa., 1952, (93 pp). See also *The Biblical Basis of Infant Baptism,* Dwight Harvey Small, Revell, 1959.

infant baptism and at the place of spiritual preparation for receiving communion—at both these places where the Church could strengthen herself we find the greatest weakness in practice today.

For Protestants generally the chief problem in understanding the sacraments is to understand the relationship between the sign and the thing signified. Some brief and helpful definitions have come down to us through the writings of the Churchmen and Reformers. The sacrament is "a physical sign of a spiritual reality." The sacrament is "the external sign of an inner reality." Sacraments have been called "the visible word." Just as we have an "audible word" which conveys the promises and benefits of Christ to a believer, so we have in the sacrament a "visible word" which conveys Christ and his benefits.

The problem of the sign and its content is brought into sharp focus in the words of the institution of the Lord's Supper—"This *is* my body." What shall be done with that word "is?" Does the sentence make an equation between the sign and the body of Christ? Is the bread actually the body, the cup the blood, in any literal sense? Christendom has been rocked by arguments over this brief verse and its meaning in the sacrament.

The Romanists, for example, make of this sentence an equation. They introduce a term, "transubstantiation," which seems like a difficult word but which breaks easily into the ideas which they wish to convey.

They argue that in the miracle of the Mass the *substance* of Christ crosses over (trans-substance) to become the *substance* of the bread. The bread, of course, does not change in appearance or in taste, but such qualities, they argue, are accidental and have nothing to do with the *substance* of the bread. If we can look at material in this fashion, made up of substance and accidents (the accidents are those changeable qualities available to the five senses) then we can at least understand, if not accept, what the Romanists are describing as happening in the Mass. Now the *substance* of the bread *is* the substance of *Christ*. The Reformers sensed idolatry at the heart of this view, for idolatry is fundamentally the confusion of the created world with the Creator, and when the priest handles the bread, is he handling the very substance of Christ? This is also what the communicant takes and eats.

Luther had a real dilemma. As a Reformer he wanted to protect the Scripture, the literality of Scripture if possible. He refused to accept what he thought was the idolatry of transubstantiation, but he could not let go of the words, "This *is* my body." He tried to solve the problem with what was called "consubstantiation." No equation is made between the bread and Christ, but the explanation is that in the miracle of the Lord's Supper Christ is present in *substance* "in, around, and under" the substance of the bread. There is no identification of the bread with Christ but there is no way one can take the bread without taking

Christ. A good illustration is in the heating of iron. The Lutheran rightly points out two things: the heat and the iron are not the same thing, not the same sort of thing, and are not identified; on the other hand, it is impossible to take any portion of the iron in which you do not at the same time take the heat. The heat is always "in, around, and under" the iron. Thus Luther held to the literality of the words, "This is my body," without introducing idolatry, i.e., the confusion of creature and Creator.

The interpretation of Calvin and the Calvinistic churches rests on the symbolic use of the statement, "This is my body." Zwingli was willing to allow this sentence to be nothing but a figure of speech: "This represents my body." He then threw the weight of the interpretation on the words "in remembrance of me." Calvin, however, was insistent that the problem of the words, "This *is* my body" could not be evaded by a retreat to the idea of remembrance alone. He believed in the symbolism of the words but he also believed in the content of the symbols. The symbolism must not be an empty symbolism. The elements in the Lord's Supper are not "nude" signs. What Calvin finally argued for was the presence of Christ in the elements; it is not *physical* but *real* presence. How is such an interpretation to be understood? How are these symbolic elements to be thought of as "physical signs of spiritual realities"?

Think for a moment about symbolism in general,

the symbolism of the American flag, for example. The stripes stand for the original thirteen colonies, the stars for the states, and the colors of the flag all have their own significances. No one says that the flag does any more than represent these things; no one says that the flag *is* the United States of America. But at the same time the symbolism is so close that the flag is always treated with respect, men doff their hats when it passes in parade, and we could have a riot if someone should trample the flag purposely or degrade it in any way. We all know, of course, for everyone knows this, that the flag is only material, the stuff of which flags are made. But is it *only* material if we take our hats off to it?

Try a closer symbolism than that of a flag. If you want directions from me for a trip from Pittsburgh to Miami, I can show you a map on which the two cities and the highways between are indicated. I say to you, as we discuss your trip, "Now this is Pittsburgh and this is Miami and this is Route 19 where you start out." The word "is" has crept into our natural conversation. Neither of us believes that the mark on the map "is" Pittsburgh and that another mark on a map "is" Miami. The language, however, is significant in showing that the word "is" does not force an equation or literal usage. Unless you accept from me the close relationship between the sign and the thing signified which is reflected in my speech, you cannot follow my directions from Pittsburgh to Miami.

Calvin gets an even closer symbolism in the illustration of two men shaking hands over an agreement. We see the sign—the handshake—and when we see the sign we know that the agreement has been made, the agreement being made not in the handshake but in the minds and hearts of the men who are doing the handshaking. The agreement is the unseen reality and the handshaking is the sign. The handshake is "the visible sign of an invisible reality." When we see one we know the other is there, and each party to the handshake receives the agreement through the sign between them. Or take the signature on a check. The check is given full value in the purchase of a house or of a car. The signature is a "sign and a seal" so that value is conveyed by means of the check when that sign and seal of the signature is there. The check has no value, no content, until the signature is there. The sign conveys the content.

So it is with the signs of the sacraments. The signs are simple elements only. According to God's promise, however, and according to the mental and spiritual condition of the person receiving the sign, when we see the sign, or receive the sign, or have the sign applied to us, we can be sure that the thing signified is really there. In Calvinism we do not say that Christ or his promises are *physically* there, but we do say that they are *really* there. The realities are spiritual realities. Just as the handshake was a true sign of an agreement which was in no sense physical but in every sense real, so in a sacrament we have true signs and seals which communicate to believers the promised realities.

It is a common question: "But isn't Christ always present in the heart of the believer?" Yes, by all means. In the sacrament the difference lies, not in the fact of his presence, but in *the intensity of the experience* of his presence. This is not a difference in kind but in degree. I remember seeing a young woman displaying her engagement ring to a friend with the greatest happiness and pride. Why did she ever want an engagement ring? What was there about a ring which made her happy? What did she have with the ring which she didn't have without the ring? She knew perfectly well that the young man loved her and wanted to marry her; she had heard many audible words about this. But her ring was a "visible" word. The ring brought into focus and intensity what was always true of his love. She used the sign "to show forth" the reality, to make the truth real in a new way at a new center of attention. We are always surrounded by sunlight but a sun glass can bring the rays into sharp focus at one point and when that happens something lights up!

God in his infinite wisdom and infinite goodness knows our finiteness and our finite needs. As a means of grace he has ordained the sacraments, so that he may convey as he portrays in sensible ways his presence and his promises.

Chapter Thirteen

THE SECOND ADVENT

AT THE TIME OF JESUS' ASCENSION, THE DISCIPLES WHO had gathered there with him were given this word of assurance: "This Jesus, who was taken up from you into heaven, will come in the same way as you saw him go into heaven." As a result of this promise with added material drawn from the Gospels and the Epistles, it has been the belief of the Church that Jesus will return again and that his return will be a physical appearing, this time in power; that he will be with his people and will rule over them.

The fact of the second advent has been colored by the question of the timing of the second advent. Another word is always relevant here. It is found in the book of Revelation, chapter 20, verses 4 and 5. "They came to life again, and reigned with Christ a thousand years. The rest of the dead did not come to life again until the thousand years were ended." The period of time there referred to as "the thousand years" is called the millennium. Using this verse along with others—chiefly in Daniel, in the Olivet discourses in Matthew, and in the "Man of Sin" passages in Second Thessalonians—many Christians have busied themselves with working out a time schedule governing the coming again of our Lord.

Whereas there has been almost universal agreement on the fact of Christ's Second Coming, there has been no such agreement on the time and circumstances of his coming. In fact, the question of the timing of Christ's return has been a reason for very serious divisions among Christians and, sometimes, occasion for great bitterness. It is because of these divisions and the bitterness which they engender that many preachers and teachers of the Word have been hesitant to preach about or discuss the Second Advent. This is unfortunate and is, indeed, unsound, for the Bible abounds in verses and paragraphs, even discourses and parables from our Lord, which center on the Second Advent. To refuse to preach on or to discuss such a subject just because of its difficulty or because it has become an irritant in some quarters, is to be untrue to the Bible message, the whole counsel of God. It is possible, as we hope to show, to draw out helpful teachings from the Second Advent, even when we admit at the outset as we will at our conclusion that the time schedule has many parts in it which are at present unknown or misunderstood.

There have been three main positions among Christians as they have tried to be true to all the Bible material having to do with the timing of Christ's return. The first position is called the *Pre-Millennial View*. Accepting the verses in Revelation which refer to the thousand years either as literal or at least as indicating a fixed and perfect period of time, those who hold to the Pre-Millennial view believe that this millennium period will be ushered in by the return of Christ. In other words, they are Pre-Millennial because they believe that Christ will return *before* the millennium and that his return will usher in the millennium. With good Scriptural support, they reason that since the world is far from being in a saved condition now, and since the return of Christ is described so frequently in Scripture as imminent—that is, he could return right now, even with the world unsaved —then it follows that if he should return right now, which we have every reason to suspect if not expect, he would have to usher in the millennium of the good life on this good earth because it has certainly not arrived as yet by any other means.

These "Pre-Mills" also observe and make considerable use of the fact that whereas the world seems to be getting better and better in some directions as if pointing to the arrival of a millennium, it is also getting worse and worse in other directions; the very discoveries which seem to make for progress usually have within them the seeds of their own destruction and decay. The planes which can carry the vaccines to some isolated community of Eskimos can also let loose the hydrogen bomb whose fallout will reach to that same isolated community which we are so anxious to help. We have learned how to check polio and with equal rapidity have learned how to bring about the mass destruction of the very children whom all love and whom all would save. One observes also that evil is so entrenched, so inter-laced in the matrix of societies, and so constantly and subtly successful, that only the Lordship of a Christ returning in power seems equal to the task of saving the situation as we now face it.

A second position which is widely held is called the *Post-Millennial View*. Taking the millennium as the starting place, these Christians believe that we should put greater emphasis on the requirements of the Bible which demand social justice, the elimination of such evils as slavery, war, slums and disease, and greater emphasis on the sacrificial work of all Christians which can bring the millennium to pass. They believe also that when Christ went away the Holy Spirit, according to promise, came to be with us. He will "guide you into all truth." "Greater works than these shalt thou do because I go to the Father." It is the belief of the "Post-Mills," therefore, that with the enlightenment and empowerment of the Holy Spirit we have the work of another person of the Trinity, one surely conveying the power of God himself to us, and that with his guidance and his power we may continue to move toward the millennium. After the millennium has ar-

rived—again the good life on this good earth so enthusiastically portrayed by all the prophets—and after
the millennium has run its course, Christ himself will
return to judge and then to rule forever and ever.

The third position is called the *A-Millennial View*
and seems to have gained wide acceptance in our day.
We are not concerned here with those who might think
of themselves as "A-Mill" just because they have no
view on the millennium at all. We have to do with
those who seriously accept the fact of Christ's Second
Advent but believe that the period of time known as the
millennium is, as a period of time at least, irrelevant.

Finding the idea of the millennium mentioned only
once in Scriptures, and then in the book of Revelation
where much of the language is poetic and figurative and
where numbers especially are subject to all kinds of
interpretations, the "A-Mills" by-pass the idea of any
millennium at all and proceed to other matters. Their
picture seems to be this: the world does get better and
the world does get worse. From time to time this move
in two directions at once, toward the evil and toward
the good, demands some marked solution to the tension; some event or series of events breaks the tension,
resolves the dilemmas and gives everyone a new start.
This is something like Toynbee's theory of history in
which he sees series of challenges met by equal and opposite responses followed by crashing resolutions of the
tensions and the rise of a new challenge to which there
is a new response. The "A-Mills" recognize this series

of events in which this sort of thing repeats itself over and over again as kingdoms rise and fall, and movements ebb and flow, but they also hold to a final apocalyptic crash in history when Christ will return in the flesh, there will be the final judgment, and the life which then and there begins will be the everlasting and eternal life which has been promised. Some who hold to the A-Millennial view agree that if there is such a thing as a millennium then that period of time was already ushered in by Christ's first advent; others hold that the idea of the millennium as a perfect period of time for a perfect kind of life may well be descriptive of the life of felicity which is ushered in with Christ's return and which will continue forever and ever. To them the idea of a thousand years is just a figurative way of speaking of the perfect and complete life of the ages.

Each of these views, it seems to me, has elements of strength and weakness; none is final and complete. We should not expect finality because people who take the question of the millenium seriously at all are usually those who have a high view of the inspiration and authority of Scripture. Since such people find such divergence of opinion we should conclude that here, if any place, we see through a glass darkly.

The "Pre-Mills" are true to two elements in Scripture. They are true, first of all, to the imminence of Christ's return. "Watch, therefore," becomes their motto. No man knows the day nor the hour. The return can be like the coming of a thief in the night. We live constantly under the promise of the next event on the Divine Calendar—the return of our Lord. It is impossible to "bow out" this idea of imminence in Scripture. In the second place, these "Pre-Mills" take the first and most natural interpretation of the millennium and of those verses in the prophetic books of both Old and New Testament which speak of the good life on this good earth. They expect that when Christ ushers in the millennium there will indeed be the good life on this planet. They see no reason for minimizing this great mass of promise. Where else, then, than in the millennium can this life be lived? Who can get such a life started for all men except our Lord himself?

There is, however, one perilous flaw in the "Pre-Mills" position. They are forced to arrange for two days of judgment, one at the time of our Lord's return, and another when the millennium is finished. When they have to re-arrange the Scriptures to allow for two judgment days they fall into all kinds of schemes and all kinds of weird problems. Now we begin to hear about the pre-rapturists and the post-rapturists, the praetorists and the futurists, with a constant slide toward the more amazing and complex schedules of hyper-dispensationalism. The necessity for scheduling two judgment days opens up a whole Pandora's box of endless speculation and argument.

In the "Post-Mill" position there are also elements of strength. Like the "Pre-Mills" they take seriously the Scriptural passage which introduces the concept of the millennium, the thousand years. They also take very seriously the commands of Christ for feeding the hungry and clothing the naked. They take seriously the work of the Holy Spirit and believe that empowered and directed by Him we can continue to progress toward the millennium. They also believe the prophetic utterances about every man under his own vine and fig tree, the trees of the fields clapping their hands for joy, the lion and the lamb lying down together; all those wonderful words about the good life right here on this good earth. On the other hand, however, they have nothing to say on the imminence of Christ's return. It seems to me impossible to observe our own day in history and believe in these two truths at the same time: Christ's return can happen at any moment, that is, it is imminent; and, there is time to work our way toward the millennium. We cannot have and not have sufficient time at the same time!

The "A-Mills" are true to what we observe so frequently in our reading of history—the way in which apocalyptic judgments seem to fall on men and events, absorbing the impossible tensions of antithetical forces, resolving events into new syntheses, giving humanity a fresh start. They believe that by this process we shall eventually move to the great event when history itself shall be finished. They are also sound in seeing that in their particular view there is a place for the immediate return of Christ, the imminence idea, believing as against the "Posts," that we do not need to wait for life to reach a millennial level before Christ can break in to rule with finality and power. There is much to be said of this position until we notice that there has been an evasion of the key idea of the millennium itself. The problem is solved by eliminating it. They find it convenient to allegorize clean out of existence the verses about the millennium, and even more seriously the mass of prophetic passages on the good life here on this planet. They tend, most of them, to project the solution of our problems to a day called "beyond history." They do, however, insist on only one great Day of Judgment and thereby eliminate many difficulties to which other interpreters are subject.

When you come on this whole subject of the Second Coming, and especially the endless speculation of the timing of the Second Coming, your first reaction is one of weariness or even of half-humorous disgust. These people can't be serious about all this sort of thing; so you are tempted to judge. But it is worth noting that these people *are* serious, very serious. This discussion is never entered into except by people who take what Scripture says very seriously. The first requirement of any man who will take the time to discuss the Second Coming is that he be a serious, sincere, Bible-believing Christian. No others can get themselves agitated about the problem at all. Perhaps recognizing that those who do discuss this are concerned for the truth of Scripture will keep all of us from being too argumentative and divisive. Whatever our views, keeping the Bible at the center as our only final authority ought, at least, to keep the subject open, and give us some assurance that with more understanding of many things which we evidently do not now understand, we can move toward greater areas of agreement.

Within this context of a serious view of the Scripture, there are other factors which make important some view of the Second Coming. A man's view here will usually color his whole approach to Christian evangelism or Christian service. If a man is a "Pre-Mill" he will likely be more interested in personal evangelism than in social reform. The time is shortened and he must get the Gospel out to as many different people as possible before it is too late. Men must be "plucked out of the burning," one by one and as many as possible, and as soon as possible. The "Pre-Mill" will tend to minimize social reform, not because he does not believe in it, but because in his view of the imminence of Christ's return he is trying to put first things first. Social reform will have to wait, in case there is time to wait.

A "Post-Mill" will throw his emphasis (and we speak, by necessity in very general terms in these matters) on the side of the social gospel. He believes, of course, in personal evangelism, just as the "Pre-Mill" believes in the social application of the Gospel, but he believes with great compassion that men must be fed and clothed and housed, if only to fulfill the compassion of Christ for all of suffering humanity. We see here the conflict of what has been known as the "passion for souls" and the "compassion for the suffering." How shall men at this point have the "mind of Christ?"

The "A-Mill" usually is a man of strong convictions on election and predestination. He knows, as we all know, that our times are in God's hands. We can work for a better day and ought to; we can evangelize men personally, and we ought to; and when the number of the elect is filled, Christ will return. The "A-Mills" will evangelize and also work for the new day, knowing perhaps two things: that the millennium will not come because of their efforts, and that all men will not be saved regardless of their efforts. Apparently neither the perfect society nor the salvation of all men is within the purposes of God. In any case, they are under orders to have "passion" and "compassion"; the issues are in the hands of God; history will be fulfilled according to plans which are quite unknown to us.

Thus what a man thinks about the *timing* of the Second Coming will color his emphasis in Christian witness and service. If I were personally forced to take a position, my position would be that of the "Pre-Mill." Happily I am not forced to take such a stand. The major denominations have not seen fit—because I think they are actually unable—to state finally and officially their positions on the Second Coming. On this subject good Christians have good reasons to disagree and no man can hold any position without recognizing, in all honesty, the surds and indigestibles. The Bible may well be teaching another position which has not yet found expression and agreement among believers. It is certain, in the present state of our understanding, that there is no position without quite evident weaknesses.

We can teach and preach that Christ will come again. He will come again in a physical and powerful way. He will come in judgment and in promise. What we really need to consider is whether we are among those who "love his appearing." We shall "love his appearing" only if we are ready for his appearing. We can be ready for his judgment only if we have accepted his grace. He is coming for his own; the only question, therefore, is whether we belong to Him.

Chapter Fourteen

THE RESURRECTION: HIS
AND OURS

THE RESURRECTION OF JESUS CHRIST, AND, ON THAT BASIS,
the resurrection of all men, is central to the teaching
of the early Church. The teaching is reflected in the
sermons recorded in the Book of the Acts and in the
letters of the Apostles, especially those of the Apostle
Paul. The Resurrection of Jesus Christ and therefore the
assurance of our own resurrection are fundamental in
the doctrines of the Christian Church today.

What the early Church was maintaining, and what
the Church still maintains, is the resurrection of the
body. The resurrection of the body is written into every
basic creed of Christendom. We must keep reminding
ourselves that the idea of this kind of Resurrection was
as amazing to the early believers as it is to us. The note
of the Easter message is one of breathlessness. Men and
women throughout the whole account are running—

running to tell the amazing miracle, running to see if it can possibly be true. The early disciples knew, as we know, that there are many other possible explanations and interpretations of the general idea of a resurrection. They had heard the argument that the important thing is that a man's influence continues to live in his friends and loved ones and that this influence can be large or small, good or bad, depending on the kind of life a man lives before his death. They had heard of the possibility of re-incarnation whereby a person can come back to life again in another form or in another person and so on eternally. Plato and his followers had already made a case for the immortality of the soul as apart from the body. It would have been easy for them to have suspected, especially after the chicanery surrounding Christ's trials, that here again there is hoax or perjury or just unfortunate hallucination. The believers in the first Resurrection were first of all unbelievers. The idea of a bodily resurrection is highly incredible and so it was to them.

It was not, however, because these men and women had heard of influence or reincarnation or hallucination that they kept running back and forth checking and double-checking. These old speculations, known for centuries to anyone conversant with Greek thought, were not in the message which sent the disciples out to preach the wonder of the Resurrection fact to an unbelieving world. Their message was this, plain as a pikestaff: if a man die he shall live again. Christ with the

[184]

prints of the nails and with the wound in his side—that Christ with that body—had arisen. He had arisen indeed! And if Christ lives, we shall live. This was the message, the message of life over death, the message which threw to one side our easy unbeliefs. It was because of that message and the reality on which it was based that men could now find real victory over their sins, could live now the abundant life, could live in the blessed hope of immortality. To the age-old question, "If a man die shall he live again?" the Church of Jesus Christ came forward with the plain answer, "Yes!" There are, as we have suggested already, men and women who find this quite unbelievable. But we must never by such easy doubts be drawn into the shadows of some kind of half belief. Christianity maintains fervently and basically and against all unbelief that the resurrection of the body is really true. "We believe in the resurrection of the body."

The New Testament is filled with the message of the Resurrection; the *locus classicus* of the doctrine and the argument about the doctrine is in Paul's first letter to the Corinthians, chapter 15. The whole chapter is an *apologia,* an argumentative support of the Resurrection. By mastering the contents of that chapter, one will have the "case" for the Resurrection. In this treatment here we can indicate only the general approach and the major statements of Paul's argument.

Paul's first appeal is to people who already believe the Scriptures and we must remember that for Paul "the Scriptures" were the writings of the Old Testament alone; he was among those, and in this Corinthian passage, who were still in the process of writing the New Testament. He argues, first, therefore, that Christ rose from the dead "according to the Scriptures." Having set that down quite plainly for those who believe the Old Testament, he goes on to give a series of eye-witness accounts which were abroad in his own day and which could be examined by those who wanted further proofs. We have in the four Gospels and in this summation by Paul, ten different events pointing in witness to the Resurrection fact. Of the ten, Paul uses seven in his account in First Corinthians, making much, as one would expect, of the one appearance known personally to him—Christ's appearance to him on the Damascus Road. In two of Paul's great defenses before the Roman authorities as we have the account in Acts, and now here again in Corinthians, Paul underlines this experience of his of the Risen Christ. Paul's encounter with the Lord on the Damascus Road must never have been very far from his consciousness. It made for him a firm foundation and an assured point of departure in all his teaching and in his courageous tireless mission enterprise. But notice: in recording these Resurrection appearances, including his own, Paul is building up what we now know as the New Testament case for believing in the Resurrection. Thus his argument for belief in the Resurrection is primarily Bible-based. "The Bible says," is by Paul considered good reason for belief. Christ rose from the dead "according to the Scriptures," both Old and New Testament Scriptures, and for some people this is quite enough. "It stands written!" If we believe the Bible, how can we dis-believe the Resurrection fact. Happy are those who can bring the argument to rest at this point.

But it is perfectly evident to Paul as it is to us now, that there are many many people who do not accept the witness of the Bible. Maybe they suggest the Bible truth rests on the Resurrection fact instead of the Resurrection fact resting on the truth of the Bible. Just as Jesus was willing to have a showdown with Thomas and his intellectual doubts, so Paul is willing to face the doubts of his contemporaries as we must face ours. May we repeat again that the Resurrection fact is difficult to believe in any generation, Paul's or ours? Paul thus turns to give serious attention to the problems of unbelief. He is willing to meet people where they are with their doubts; in our approach these days we must be willing to do the same thing in so far as we are able. In every generation of church history, "Apologetics" has been that branch of theological discipline given over to our reasons for believing, prepared to meet men on their own grounds and to bring them over, so far as arguments serve, to the Christian grounds for belief. Observe, briefly, then Paul's use of apologetic.

From the twelfth to the nineteenth verses of the

fifteenth chapter of I Corinthians, Paul argues in what seems at first a very strange way. The method is termed by some "Negative Pragmatism." We need not remember the term, but we do need to understand the approach. Notice how negative the approach is. "If Christ be *not* risen, then is our preaching *vain,* and your faith is also *vain.*" Paul has already maintained that Christ has risen. But if he has not risen, then is our preaching vain and our faith futile. Paul is really arguing his statement backwards. Your preaching is not vain, your faith is not vain; therefore Christ must be risen. This kind of approach seems stronger the more you think about it. Think of the preaching of the Risen Lord wherever it has gone, all across the world and down through the centuries. Has that preaching been in vain? Indeed not. The preaching of the Risen Lord has brought new life and great fruitage wherever it has been released. Read the statement backwards, then: our preaching has not been vain, therefore it stands on the foundation of a Christ risen; on that basis the preaching has had content and life.

And what about faith? "If Christ be not risen . . . your faith is also vain." Has faith been vain all these years? Faith in other things has often proven to be vanity, but faith in the risen Lord has brought changed lives, newness of life, great victory—victory even over the sting of death. Something else can be said of faith here also. Our faith in truth itself or the possibility of truth will have a terrible shaking if Christ has not risen from the dead. Where could the Lord of the universe have been if he had allowed the cruel death of the cross to go unanswered or as the final answer? What can a man believe about the universe and the Ruler of the universe where nothing happens after the cross? Or again why should we be interested in truth at all if everything we know arising out of the Resurrection could have been based on a lie? We should set ourselves to discover other lies instead of other truths if all the glories of the history of the church have been founded on lies and on men and women who were lying about the very one whom they claimed as Truth, their Master and Lord, the whole meaning of life for them. Our whole pattern of faith —faith in truth, faith in goodness, faith in the kind of thing which sent the disciples to martyrdom in great victory—all this faith and all this kind of faith would be vanity. It is not vanity; we walk in that kind of faith every day we live. If that kind of faith is not vain, then Christ must be risen.

With the same method of argument, Paul points out that if Christ be not risen we are "yet in [our] sins." And yet those who believe in the Resurrection are the very ones who do find victory over sin. Or hear this: if we have believed in Christ only in this present life, we are "of all men most miserable." Are we? Witness victorious lives, at home and in our world mission. Are Christians the miserable ones—*real* Christians, I mean—Christians who have been enabled to believe in the Resurrection? Christians everywhere have found the deep abiding joy of the abundant life; they are of all men most joyful, and this in spite of circumstances which may surround them. "Count it all joy, brethren, when you fall into manifold temptations (trials)." It is Paul, writing from prison, who can say, "Rejoice, again I say rejoice . . . rejoice with joy unspeakable." On what foundation is such joyful possibility based? The Resurrection! Our preaching is not in vain; we have victory over sin; our faith is not vain; we are of all men, not most miserable but most victorious. Why? Because Christ has risen and all things are possible in the power of the Risen Lord.

It is on the basis of Christ's Resurrection that Paul then establishes ours. Christ is the "firstfruits," and we who are buried with him will also rise with him. Union with Christ, the Risen Christ, is the assurance of our own resurrection. No man can be in any wise dead who is *in* Him.

Of great interest to the Corinthian Church, and of equal interest to us, is the manner of the Resurrection. Paul's discussion of this begins with verse 35 in this same fifteenth chapter. What Paul is appealing to here is the easy way in which we accept all kinds of life and all kinds of bodies and still stumble over the possibility of a resurrection life and a resurrection body. There are many kinds of flesh—animal, fish, fowl. There are all kinds of bodies—terrestial and celestial. There is also a resurrection body.

Modern man should have an easier time with the resurrection body than did the believers in the early Church. What, after all, are our bodies? Certainly not the solid, material masses we usually think them to be. They are really nothing more, although that's a-plenty, than electrons in motion. We are collections of elements, the elements are structures of protons and electrons; this is the ordinary view of the experts of our day on our extraordinary structures. But what is the pattern around which these elements gather, around which these electrons do their spinning? All this dynamic activity does its spinning around a basic pattern and that basic pattern is *me*. (Bad English often makes the matter clear!) As I come to understand my own body I recognize that this body of mine has already completely died many times during the course of my life. Some scientists say that every cell of the body dies and is replaced every seven years; some say it takes eight years for the complete process. The death and replacement are all governed by different rates of growth and decay in different cells, and the changes take place quite subtly, imperceptibly in most cases. Thus every living cell in my body, in its own time and according to its own nature has died and been sloughed off into oblivion and has been replaced with a new living cell over and over again. I think nothing of this process. Every time I take a bath, dead cells go down the drain. I rub myself briskly with a towel and more cells are gone. I watch the wear and tear of calluses on my hands, cut my hair and nails which are fastened in living tissue at one end and have died at the other end. But every time I eat, new cells are formed—formed of stuff, elemental stuff, stuff gathered from all over the earth. We used to play a game in our home as children, discovering where all the food had come from which we found on the table at meal time. This kind of thinking can be educational to children but it can be educational to adults as well, as they contemplate the real nature of these bodies which they keep on feeding, and wonder about the *person* whose body is thus formed and preserved.

The wonder of this whole process is that this elemental stuff which is gathered from anywhere on any occasion still shapes itself around the core of being which is *me*. My body continues to be recognizable as mine and not yours; my thoughts are empowered to continue themselves according to *my* kind of thinking. I am constantly new and different, made as I am of the dust of the earth, the elemental stuff which I continue to ingest, but my friends recognize me every step of the way. No matter what I eat for dinner I can still pick up my same book after dinner and *I* go right on reading. This wonderful process is most vividly revealed to us in what we call adolescence. Watch your teen-ager. He has a new body, new powers, new interests, new releases from the things which bound him to childhood. Yet he continues in some sense to be the same person. He is being "clothed upon" with a new and now a mature body. He is certainly in some sense a new creature and he is still at the same time the same person. The center of his pattern of life, the pattern around which all his electrons keep buzzing—his soul, if you like—is the core of his being, around which his new body centers and in which he has his own personal identity.

What is promised to us in the resurrection is that we too shall be "clothed upon" with a "resurrection body," with a "spiritual body." We are not promised a disembodied spirit. Never! We are not to be wraiths or ghosts or spirits in that sense at all. What we are promised is that we ourselves—our identity, our core of being—will be clothed upon with a "spiritual *body*." What that body shall be is not described to us because it cannot be described to us in terms which we can understand. We do not have the vocabulary, the analogies, the experiences, by which we could be made familiar with such a body. Perhaps it would be like explaining our own bodies now in terms which the physicists have taught us to some native tribe who has no knowledge of physics and wouldn't believe that talk about electrons and protons unless you could show them a few. Our own understanding and hope for this new life should not be crippled by the limitations of our present knowledge of the unknown world. When our oldest daughter was only eight years old, she asked us one time, "What is a date?" Can you define or describe a date? How will you define it to an eight-year-old? Now ten years later she doesn't even ask the question, and so we are not under the necessity of defining something to someone who has grown into a new life where that sort of thing is in itself perfectly clear. The time when it couldn't be explained has been replaced by a time when it needn't be explained. With a new body, new powers, new perspectives, the post-adolescent doesn't have to ask the questions which plague the pre-adolescent. There are things which can be explained to us only in terms with which we have had some experience. The resurrection body is the promise of a brand new experience, something beyond what we could even ask or think.

Even so, there are some things we can say about the resurrection body. In some way it will be like Christ's resurrection body described by his resurrection experiences. This is not a full description; it is description only by illustration and event. He seems to have had victory over time and space and was not stopped by the solidity (so-called) of material things. The resurrection life is also to be free from sin and the ravages of sin; it will be free from pain and anxiety; it will be free from death and the sting of death. Judging from the interesting piece of work God has done in the creation of this life which I now enjoy, I believe I can trust him with the creation of the next life. His hand is in no way shortened by our short imaginations; his love has thought of a lot of things which will surprise us; his promises about this sort of thing are only suggestions and hints now but they are promises inter-locked with what he has already shown us in Christ. What is of chief importance to Christians is that "we shall be like Him." That should be enough to think about now. And as Paul ends his treatment of the sub-ject in the fifteenth chapter of First Corinthians we can follow his lead: "this corruptible *must* put on in-corruption." Death is a "must," a necessity for entrance into that newness of life. "Therefore," these things being our hope, "be ye steadfast, unmovable, always abound-ing in the work of the Lord, forasmuch as ye know that your labor is not in vain in the Lord."

Chapter Fifteen

CHRISTIAN FAITH AND LIFE

"FAITH," SAYS THE WRITER TO THE HEBREWS, "IS THE substance of things hoped for, the evidence of things not seen." Many have memorized this definition and say it very easily, perhaps too easily. It is the sort of definition which requires the most profound study and it is not likely to have full understanding even in a lifetime of meditation; its interrelationships and repercussions are as surprising as they are countless. In our consideration of faith and life, however, we must lay hold on this definition (it is the classic one) and make it a starting place, at least, for our understanding.

Look at the definition again and see what a strange definition it is. This word "faith" operates in two worlds at the same time. "Faith" has to do with "things hoped for" and "things unseen." As such, it operates in the ideal, unseen, hoped-for world out there in front of us, somewhere in the undefined future. At the same

[196]

time faith has to do with things which are now happening, because faith is "substance" and "evidence."

We know "substance" and "evidence" through our five senses. A man of our day prides himself in being realistic in his approach to life; he is always thinking very plainly and matter-of-factly in terms of substance and evidence. On the other hand when a man turns out to be idealistic about life, he is trying to think in terms of what might be, what could be, things hoped for and unseen. The so-called "realistic" thinker is apt to judge the idealist as a dreamer. He is not dealing with real things but nebulous things. Yet here is our definition of faith operating in both of these worlds. Faith, in the clearest way, is a two-world word, operating *at the same time* in the substance and evidence of this world of time and space so dear to the realistic thinker, and in the unseen and hoped-for world of the idealist and dreamer.

The writer to the Hebrews expands his thesis after he gives us this definition in Hebrews 11 by describing men and women of faith as men and women of action— always they are people who were doing something or had done something. Faith, in spite of its other-worldly point of reference, operates very much in this world. It is when we try to separate these two worlds of operation that we lose the right understanding of faith. There are people who allow themselves some kind of rest and satisfaction in the nebulous world of the hoped for and unseen. They may sharpen this world a little by explanations and definitions, but for one reason or another, they never get into the world of action with what they call their faith. They believe a great many things, many of which are certainly true, but belief is never put to work. On the other hand there are those who work very hard right here and right now and frequently with great understanding and compassion, but they lose power and meaning and a sense of direction because they never line up what they are doing with the hoped for, unseen, ideal world: the other side of their faith.

"We walk by faith," means that, whether we will or not, we have to have faith in something or someone to have any way of getting started at all. Even when we do something as simple as the walking out of a room, we walk into the next room which up to the time we pass through the door has been completely hoped for and unseen. The very fact of our walking gives substance and evidence to our belief that the other room is still there and can be entered. Some years ago, while serving as Dean of Men at Grove City College, I began to sense that one type of problem coming to my office was taking on a kind of pattern. Usually the problem boy was a sophomore, he still had no choice of vocation, he had lost some of the excitement of being a freshman, the newness of things was wearing off, he was beginning to edge into trouble which might develop into real trouble. There were irritations in the dormitory, words of warning from professors, letters from anxious parents. What we usually discovered was that this boy had lost, or had never possessed, a "sense of direction." Our problem was to give him this much-needed "sense of direction." How? We had to discover for him or better get him to discover for himself some point of reference far beyond his college days, some ambition, some dream or vision. Nebulous stuff, those dreams and visions. Nevertheless, if we could get him to lay hold on something "way out there," some amazing things could happen right now and here. Let the dream of being a great surgeon or a C.P.A. or a trial lawyer get hold of him and his life would get straightened out. Faith was doing its work; things hoped for and unseen were now being given substance and evidence. Putting into action some dream which would not be fulfilled for many years made out of the boy now a "new creature," or should we say of a college boy a "new ciittur!"

Another example which has always helped me to understand this can be observed at any dog show in any of our larger communities. Men and women bring their pure-bred dogs to the show and there have them judged for their perfections. Let us suppose that a man has been breeding boxers. Perhaps to his wife's great distress, he has been spending his spare money on his hobby of raising boxers. He has been very definitely spending his "substance," and there is "evidence" in everything he does of his great dream—the dream of producing a prize-winning boxer. Through several generations of boxers, he has been breeding toward perfection, and he has "acted" on the basis of an ideal boxer, which is still the kind of dog "hoped for"— still a "thing unseen." Notice, please, that no one has ever seen a perfect boxer; even a man who spends his life breeding boxers has never seen a perfect boxer. Toward what then is this man breeding? He is breeding toward a perfect animal which is "hoped for" and "unseen." And I repeat, in his actions, in his works, he gives substance and evidence of the things hoped for and still unseen.

Finally one night he leads his boxer into the ring, and his dog is judged the best boxer in the show. The judging of the best boxer is as wondrous as has been the breeding of the boxer in the first place, for the same sort of thing goes on again: the judges in the ring pass judgment on this boxer and the other boxers according to an ideal boxer which all the breeders know is still "hoped for" and "unseen." The dog is judged to have the best points only because there is general agreement about what a boxer *ought* to be, and that *ought* is a perfection that hasn't yet arrived on the scene here below.

Suppose, finally, that our champion boxer is now adjudged the best dog in the show—the best dog against a French poodle, a Russian wolfhound, and a Scotty. This judgment means that a great many people have presumed to know what "best" means in terms of general doggishness! It is a tremendous judgment to make to say that a boxer is found to be more perfect *as a dog* than, say, a Great Dane. Dog fanciers, apparently, can think of a perfect *dog*, regardless of breed; but we must point out again that the perfections to which they refer when judging the best dog in the show in terms of his perfect doggishness, are perfections which are still hoped for and unseen. And we must remember that with complete naturalness and great confidence we do this sort of thing when we breed horses, or cotton, or cows or pecans, when we set up institutions of higher learning or establish a form of government. Strangely, some criticize religious people because, as men and women of faith, they seem quite gullible in accepting "things hoped for" and "unseen" as the ideals and goals for the directing of their own lives.

When we move from dogs to people and when, specifically, we move to the Christian faith, we have one remarkable datum which is missing in the breeding of animals and plants. This datum constitutes one of the great basic tenets of what we call the Christian faith and it is this: when the "Word became flesh and dwelt among us," and when men saw and handled "the word of life," then that "hoped-for" and "unseen" world of man's dreams and inspirations actually appeared in Jesus Christ.

One cannot be a Christian without at least this basic fact. What God has to say about himself, he said finally in Jesus Christ; more to our point here, what God had to say about mankind, human nature, what man is supposed to be in all his marvelous potential, he said in Jesus Christ. Christ is the Alpha and Omega, the beginning and the end; in these last days God has spoken to us about the things having to do with our nature and our needs and our goals, in Jesus Christ. When as Christians we ask what a man is supposed to be, what a man ought to be, the thing "hoped for" but still "unseen" in human life, we point to the perfections of Jesus. All the promises of life are "yea and amen" in Christ Jesus.

Christian faith, therefore, in its essentials, requires that we lay hold on Jesus, or, more exactly, be laid hold on by Jesus; and the things of Christ are to begin to be operative in our lives. It is a kind of imitation of Christ; but it is much more, because in the whole process God has been the Initiator, and he is the Sustainer, and he provides the goal. In Christ God has entered into human life with the free gift of salvation made possible through the finished work of redemption. It is not yet evident what we shall be out of all this, but we shall "be like him for we shall see him as he is." In the meantime faith is the action which follows the fact that "things hoped for" and still "unseen" in our own lives are already apparent in his life, and we lay hold of such things and put them to work, or better, he lays hold of us and his life shows itself in us. And we grow from faith to faith.

In his letter to the Romans Paul makes clear to us that the life of perfection which is required of us is quite impossible to us in and of our own efforts. He makes it desperately clear that the heathen world has failed and does fail; he points up the tragedy of the high calling of the Jews and their failure. Thus with the wrath of God turned against all unrighteousness, and with the total failure of the human family to "make good," some other way had to be worked out.

Since man has no righteousness in and of himself, there is now provided "the righteousness of God" which must be given to man and received by him through faith. This fundamental act of God, which is really the perfect obedience of Christ, is offered freely as a grace gift and is received by faith. Thus, by Christ's total redemptive act—life, death, resurrection—God is now able to forgive us and to offer us his righteousness in Christ. Our faith, then, is to receive this free gift, trusting that what he has provided and promised, he will fulfill. From that point on, what we have received, the righteousness of Christ, begins its work in us. "By faith Abel . . ." did something; "by faith Abraham . . ." did something; "by faith" we begin to do something, and that something is to give substance and evidence in daily living of what has now laid hold on us, of what is yet to be in the glory which still lies ahead. In this new relationship we begin with faith and continue to grow by faith.

It is only on the basis of that faith—Christ working in and through us, the substance and evidence of things hoped for and still unseen—that we can talk of the Christian life. We are often tempted to talk of the Christian life from some man-made starting place. This may be a life including some moral victories, but it can well be a life leading in a totally wrong direction. A half-breed dog may have many of the markings of a full-bred boxer but could never be bred toward perfection. I remember standing near a casket of a man and hearing one of his friends say, "He was a good Christian; he always told the truth and paid his debts." It is true that a Christian will tell the truth and pay his debts; but this is not what constitutes his Christianity. The whole idea of "salvation by works" is getting off to that kind of a bad start.

The Christian life is a life of faith. We are in a saving relationship to God through Jesus Christ. Our works of righteousness are the *result* of this relationship, not the cause of the relationship; and in that living relationship we go from strength to strength as his life infuses ours. Christianity, therefore, is never an attainment but always a process; we can never level off at any point in Christian experience with the assurance that we have now arrived; rather we continue to walk in a relationship. Christianity is dynamic, not static; we walk with a living Lord.

Because our Christian life is all of Christ, there is in it no place for pride or judging, however great we may think our own attainments to be. The Christian life, rightly understood, is a life of humble dependence on Christ. This means that automatically there is no place for the attitude of the Pharisee; all our attainments and all our talents and all our successes are gifts initiated and sustained by the grace of God and received daily as his free gifts.

In youth work I have been worried by the way in which young people so frequently get hold of this whole idea by the wrong end. Someone has told them that they must give up things in order to be a Christian. They must quit dancing and they must quit smoking. Missionaries have been accused (falsely) of making natives wear clothes as a requirement for salvation. Not so, and never! Young people must be confronted with Jesus Christ, and by the power of the Holy Spirit, born again into a new relationship, a totally new way of looking at everything in life because of Jesus Christ. Out of this confrontation they may be led to give up certain practices which seemed normal to the old way of life, but this will happen rightly only if it happens from "the expulsive power of a new affection." There is a new relationship, not a new legalism; a new love, not a new law. Jesus Christ our Saviour leads us into the life of a saved man, through his wonderful words of life, made living in us by the Holy Spirit through Holy Writ; these new perfections are beyond and above, but never therefore apart from the law.

Rate of growth and directions of growth in individual lives may follow different patterns. One new convert may think he has to give up smoking; another may never think of it seriously for years, if at all. One may decide that he has some forgiving to do among his circle of acquaintances. Another has to go somewhere and make a public repentance. In this new relationship it is Jesus Christ who is saving us, and we are to be like him according to his direction and help, not under the approval or condemnation of our neighbor; the things of Christ hoped for and unseen must now show substance and evidence in our lives. We begin to show our faith by our works. We, who are teachers should have no yen that our students should imitate us; we can bear witness only by pointing to the One who has done great things for us. If we give advice at all it is only by way of telling what was wrong and how it was righted *in our case,* and quite evidently not by us but by Christ. We can suggest that the same sort of thing could happen for others but there is no place here for us to set down any pattern from our own successes. We are witnesses, that is, we are pointers, and we point to the Living Word who is to come alive in others as he came alive in us.

Many things in life are immediately apparent to the Christian as either right or wrong, Christian or un-Christian; and Christ's command in the Sermon on the Mount is indeed a command: "Be ye perfect." It is the command of the One to whom we have turned over our lives and our destinies. We can never play fast and loose with the commands of One we call Master. But again let it be made perfectly clear that in addition to those things which are evidently Christian or un-Christian—sacrificial giving as against murder, for example—there are many things in our complex lives and our fast-moving society for which we need more light and guidance. Men—and they were Christian men—took centuries to discover what they must do about dueling and slavery. Now we must learn lessons about segregation. We have to get some fresh starts on subjects like management and labor, war and peace. These problems of international scope are matched by personal problems within the individual life. With just one choice to be made in a lifetime and that choice to be made for a loved one, what shall we do, for example, with these pressing problems: should aged parents be kept at home or put in a home? Which of several colleges is the right one for our children? How late should a growing boy (and we are interested in his maturing), be allowed out with the family car? What advice can one give on vocation that can possibly be relevant for all possibilities twenty years from now? How does one spend his spare time? How does a pastor rightly divide his time between study, calling, administration and family? In all these things we must learn to walk by faith.

Our faith requires of us only one thing basically, that we lay hold on Jesus Christ, bring his life to bear on the things of this life, and let him lead us into all righteousness. At the same time, part of our trust will be this, that having committed our way to him we can believe that he will pick up the loose ends, cover the mistakes, restore the joy. As we truly seek His will, we can rest in faith on the decisions to which He leads us. Having put the hand to the plow we need not look back.